Starting:
Current:

EXPERIENCE POINTS: $(20 = 1$ PERMANENT LIFE POINT$)$:

EQUIPMENT

Silver Pieces $(10 = 1$ Gold Piece$)$:

From previous adventures:

SPELLS

PANIC	PIN
POW	PIR^2
PILL	INVISIBILITY
PAD	FIREFINGERS
PIP	FIREBALLS

BATTLE SCORES

Enemy:	Enemy:	Enemy:
Enemy LIFE POINTS:	Enemy LIFE POINTS:	Enemy LIFE POINTS:
Result:	Result:	Result:
Enemy:	Enemy:	Enemy:
Enemy LIFE POINTS:	Enemy LIFE POINTS:	Enemy LIFE POINTS:
Result:	Result:	Result:
Enemy:	Enemy:	Enemy:
Enemy LIFE POINTS:	Enemy LIFE POINTS:	Enemy LIFE POINTS:
Result:	Result:	Result:
Enemy:	Enemy:	Enemy:
Enemy LIFE POINTS:	Enemy LIFE POINTS:	Enemy LIFE POINTS:
Result:	Result:	Result:
Enemy:	Enemy:	Enemy:
Enemy LIFE POINTS:	Enemy LIFE POINTS:	Enemy LIFE POINTS:
Result:	Result:	Result:

The Den of Dragons is the second book of the Grailquest, a different kind of fantasy gamebook series in which YOU become the hero of thrilling adventures.

A huge and murderous dragon is on the rampage in the legendary kingdom of Avalon, leaving a trail of death and destruction in its wake. King Arthur's brave Knights of the Round Table are powerless against this terrifying creature—but YOU have been chosen to attempt what all others have failed. Your route is full of treacherous snares and fiendish creatures that you must fight and kill before they overcome you. Do you have the skill and courage to seek out and slay the hideous reptile, or will you perish within the Den of Dragons?

To play your way through this adventure gamebook you need two dice, a pencil and an eraser. Keep a record of your progress in the Quest Journal at the front of the book, and refer to the handy Rules of Combat sheet on the last page.

J. H. BRENNAN is well known in the fantasy games world. He has always been interested in magic, spells and wizardry, and among his many books has written a number of them on magic. He lives in Ireland.

ALSO AVAILABLE IN LAUREL-LEAF BOOKS:

GRAILQUEST

Book Two

The Den
of Dragons

J. H. Brennan

Illustrated by John Higgins

LAUREL-LEAF BOOKS

LAUREL-LEAF BOOKS bring together under a single imprint outstanding works of fiction and nonfiction particularly suitable for young adult readers, both in and out of the classroom. Charles F. Reasoner, Professor Emeritus of Children's Literature and Reading, New York University, is consultant to this series.

Published by
Dell Publishing Co., Inc.
1 Dag Hammarskjold Plaza
New York, New York 10017

This work was first published in Great Britain by Armada Books.

Laurel-Leaf Library ® TM 766734, Dell Publishing Co., Inc.

ISBN: 0-440-91873-1

RL: 8.3

Printed in the United States of America

December 1986

10 9 8 7 6 5 4 3 2 1

WFH

CONTENTS

MERLIN

Hallo? Hallo? Is anybody there? Can you hear me? Can you read me?

I'm speaking into a seashell. A conch shell to be exact. Four knights and a Sergeant-at-Arms think I've gone bonkers, but they know nothing about magic. No. No, indeed. When you're a Wizard like me, you can use a conch shell like a telephone (which is just as well, since telephones haven't been invented in my Time).

Hallo? Is there anybody at the other end of my conch shell? This is Camelot calling. Are you receiving me? You. Yes, YOU! The one sitting there reading that 'Grailquest' book. It's part of my magic, that book. Yes, indeed. And a very important part.

You are reading a SPELL – did you know that? I wrote it myself and sent it forward through Time in the shape of a book. It's a net spell. It catches your mind as you read the book. Nets it like a fish, I hope. Then I draw in the net, and next thing you know you're in my Time. Your mind is, anyway: your body stays more or less where it is.

You'd like to visit my Time, wouldn't you? It's

full of interesting things. Knights. Squires. Jousting. Quests. That sort of thing. It's the Time of King Arthur – the Time of Camelot and the Table Round. Or Round Table as people insist on calling it – wrongly.

I want you to visit my Time. I *need* you to visit my Time: there's a bit of a problem with dragons. Just a small thing – you'll sort it out in no time. You'll find it easy to visit. Just carry on reading this book – that's all there is to it. Turn a few pages and the spell will start to work. That isn't too hard, is it?

Nearly forgot. When you arrive you'll find you've become Pip, the adopted child of a Freeman farmer called John, and his wife Miriam. Pip's been leading a fairly quiet kind of life recently, but all that's about to change.

You'll need to bring dice with you. Ordinary six-sided dice, preferably with spots. You'll need one at least, though two would be better. You'll also need a bit of paper, something to write with, and an eraser. That's the equipment you'll need to get you started. Just go off and collect it now, before you do anything else. *Then* you can begin.

THE THREAT
TO AVALON

There was always trouble when it rained in August. The first two weeks especially. Old residenters would look up at the leaden sky and mumble grimly, 'Rain in August the first week, next year's outlook will be bleak.' And anyone who happened to overhear them would be prone to adding the second half of the ancient saw: 'And if the rain continues on, all hope of peaceful times is gone.'

Well, it *had* rained the first week of August last year. And the second. And the third. And the fourth. In fact it was still raining well into September, by which time everbody was thoroughly sick of listening to the old residenters mumbling grimly to themselves. Everybody was

Lightning blasted the Druid oak

thoroughly nervous as well. A wet start to August meant a good breeding season for dragons, which in turn meant a plague of the fire-breathers when they reached maturity the next year. The Knights of the Round Table would do their bit in killing off the pests, of course, but when there was a really good breeding season there were never enough knights to go round. So the dragons rampaged something shocking, setting thatch alight, devouring cattle, terrorising villages and carrying off maidens.

But that wasn't the only thing. Last August – the August we've been talking about – there were *Omens* as well as rain. At least, the old residenters claimed they were Omens. Lightning blasted the Druid oak on Glastonbury Common twice in succession during a particularly violent storm.

'Everybody knows lightning never strikes twice in the same place,' muttered the old residenters grimly. 'That be an Omen, that be.'

Then there was the business with the gravedigger who managed to bury himself in an open grave. When the funeral procession arrived with the coffin, there was no neat hole for it to go in; only a slight indentation filled with loose earth and beneath it the unfortunate gravedigger, now as dead as his former clients. The inquest decided it was an accident, a landslip brought on by all the rain. But the old residenters were far from satisfied.

'Old Silas would never have made a mistake like

that,' they muttered grimly, referring to the late gravedigger. 'That be an Omen, that be.'

And so it went on throughout the rainy month of August. A massive thunderstone ploughed a deep furrow through Farmer Gabriel's meadow and killed five of his sheep. A two-headed calf was born in the herd that kept the Abbey monks supplied with milk. King Arthur's favourite falcon slipped its tie and flew off southwards, never to be seen again.

And for once it turned out that the old residenters were absolutely right. The following year was absolutely dreadful. Fresh, vigorous young dragons popping up all over the Realm, with new ones appearing as fast as the harassed knights could kill the old ones off. But that wasn't the worst of it. The plague of dragons could be easily enough explained by the good breeding season occasioned by the rainy August. The Omens pointed towards something else. The old residenters waited patiently, nodding their heads grimly at each new report of dragon damage. 'That bein't the worst to come,' they would say. 'Not by a long chalk.'

The worst to come came in June, on a cloudless day that promised a long, dry summer. On the morning of that day, a carriage emblazoned with ecclesiastical insignia thundered (unannounced) up to the gates of Camelot with quite unecclesiastical indications of haste, and there emerged from it, demanding immediate audience with the King, a portly messenger from His Eminence the Archbishop of Canterbury. He was admitted at once, of course, and despite a tendency towards pomposity, managed to capture King Arthur's attention with the very first words he spoke. The words were: 'Your Majesty, a Brass Dragon has escaped from Hell.'

Now this was not, of course, precisely true. Brass Dragons were extremely rare in Avalon – or anywhere else for that matter – and there was considerable controversy about their origins. Churchmen generally believed they were bred in Hell itself and said so dogmatically whenever the subject arose in conversation. But the infernal origins of Brass Dragons had never been satisfactorily proven and there was a body of opinion which held the beasts came from somewhere else. The truth was, no one quite knew for sure. (Not even the old residenters, who thought they knew everything.) What everyone *did* know was that Brass Dragons were very bad news indeed.

A word about dragons generally may not go amiss here, since not everyone is personally familiar with the breed. Your average run-of-the-mill dragon – the sort that mates in August if it's raining – is a grey-skinned, scaled and ridged-backed reptile weighing somewhere around six tons and growing to a length of five metres. There are two main species – those that move on four feet and are fully equipped with claws, and those which move mainly by means of their two hind legs and use their shortened front legs rather like arms. The latter type, which are generally more intelligent, have claws only on the hind feet. The forefeet have developed into hands of a sort.

Both species are aggressive, vicious, and extremely difficult to kill on account of their heavy scaling which acts as natural armour. Both are meat-eaters, which accounts for the devoured cattle and probably the missing maidens. And both share the curious habit of consuming foliage from chestnut trees during the first hour and fifteen minutes after sunrise. The business with the chestnut leaves has nothing to do with hunger. Leaves consumed at this time do not travel down the normal digestive tract (which does not open until two hours after sleep) but go instead into a second stomach set forward and a little below that which the reptile uses to digest food. Here, in this second stomach, the leaves are converted into sedimentary layers of humus which, encouraged by the dragon's body heat, gives off vast quantities of methane gas.

Methane, as you probably know, is highly inflammable. What you may not know is that once a dragon is four months old, it develops crystalline extrusions on its upper fangs and a thin layer of natural metallic capping on the lower. The result of these developments is that when the dragon snaps its jaws together sharply, it produces a spark. This spark will normally ignite the almost continuous flow of methane from the second stomach, producing the fiery dragon breath which is such a distinctive feature of the breed.

All in all, dragons are very formidable creatures. But Brass Dragons make ordinary dragons look like pussycats. There have only been five authenticated appearances of Brass Dragons in the whole of recorded human history: two in Asia, one in Europe, one in Spain and one which turned up in Londinium before the Romans left. In every instance, the destruction wrought was massive. Three-quarters of Londinium was demolished or ravaged by fire, and *seventeen* of the very finest Roman Legions completely wiped out before the beast stupidly consumed the entire stock of an ale-house and drowned after falling drunkenly into the Thames.

While the natural history of the ordinary dragon is relatively well known, no one really has the least idea where Brass Dragons come from, what laws govern their abrupt appearance, or how to get rid of them when they do appear. Typically, a Brass Dragon will turn up out of the blue, run riot for several months or years, then simply disappear. (The Drowned Dragon of Londinium was unusual in the way it met its fate.) No one ever succeeded in killing one, neither knight nor commoner. One reason for this noteworthy failure is that there is every indication Brass Dragons may be magic. No wonder the Church considered they escaped from Hell.

'A Brass Dragon?' gasped King Arthur.

'A Brass Dragon?' gasped King Arthur

'Escaped from Hell,' confirmed the Archbishop's messenger grimly.

At which the pent-up tensions of the Court exploded abruptly and everybody began to talk at once, swoon, scream, run and otherwise react to the news. It was pandemonium. King Arthur had to wait for order to be restored before he heard the whole story.

First off, there was absolutely no doubt about the monster really being a Brass Dragon. Although rare, the species was quite unmistakable. For a start, they grow more than twice the size of ordinary dragons and their colour, far from grey, is a metallic brass, which glints and sparkles in the sunshine. Then there was the magic. Brass Dragons have generally been credited with all sorts of wonders, including the power of speech. No one had heard this particular Brass Dragon talk yet and its wonders were so far confined to the 'now you see it, now your don't' variety, appearing and disappearing without anybody knowing where it came from or where it went to. But this was more than enough to establish that it was magic.

The first reported sighting of the beast was near a forest close by Winchester, where it was apparently amusing itself by demolishing a woodsman's hut. The artisan who saw it had drink taken, so his story was given less credence than it might, even though the wreckage of the hut was plainly there for all to see.

The creature next turned up briefly in Cornwall (although how King Arthur, who had relatives in Cornwall, missed hearing about it was a mystery). Several fishermen, pulling out in pursuit of the day's catch, noticed it clinging to a cliff face. Since they were sober men, as sailors have to be, their word was believed, although a party of men-at-arms sent to investigate could discover not a hint of anything on or near the cliff.

There was what might have been a third manifestation far to the north where *something* (although no one could say exactly what) had torn huge holes in the remains of Hadrian's Wall, that vast rampart left by the Romans to keep the greedy Scots from marching south to sell the English whisky.

But the worst of it was the attack on Cerne Abbas Monastery, that ancient seat of learning overlooked by a very rude picture of a giant carved into a hillside in prehistoric times. It was from that very hillside that the Brass Dragon had approached. The survivors claimed it was as large as a castle, with eyes the size of soup plates and a flaming breath more than a hundred metres long. The ground shook with every step it took. Its roar was like thunder. And so on. All greatly exaggerated, no doubt, as these things tend to be, but the fact remained that Cerne Abbas Monastery was no more. The stonework was demolished as if struck down by an army of battering rams. The woodwork was burned to a cinder. All the tapestries, rush matting, curtaining and a priceless library of books, manuscripts and scrolls went up in smoke. The Abbot was burned to death trying to save a relic of the True Cross from the monastery chapel. One hundred and seventy-eight monks were trapped beneath the fallen rubble. Herds of cattle and sheep lay dead and mangled in the monastery fields. Even the kitchen garden at the back was buried under a pile of evil-smelling manure which, unlike normal manure, killed off plants rather than encouraged their growth.

Out of this whole disaster, only two young monks escaped with their lives. (They had been sent off on a ten mile hike as penance for talking in Chapel, which just goes to show it doesn't pay to be good *all* the time.) And the only artifact that was saved was a stained-glass window depicting the Holy Grail. Since this *should* certainly have been broken, its survival was seen as confirmation that the destruction was the Devil's work – the Devil being unable to harm anything as holy as the Holy Grail.

This was a catastrophe of almost unimaginable proportions and there was no doubt a Brass Dragon had been involved. Although the two young monks saw nothing of it, the creature's rampage had been witnessed (at a safe distance) by no fewer than eighty pilgrims from Londinium who were travelling to Cerne Abbas to view the same relic which had been the death of the Abbot.

When news reached the Archbishop who was usually the last to be told anything due to his fiery temper, it produced a predictable reaction. His language was so extreme that one churchwarden was heard to remark he would personally have preferred to face the dragon any day. But sharp tempers are quick to abate and the Archbishop was no fool. He realised that if a Brass Dragon *was* on the loose, something had to be done about it – and quickly. Thus, when he had regained control of himself, he dispatched a messenger to Camelot: the same messenger who now related the whole sorry tale to King Arthur. And the King, who was one of those firmly convinced Brass Dragons were magical by nature, in turn dispatched a messenger of his own. That messenger was instructed to find the Wizard Merlin.

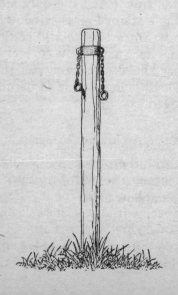

IN MERLIN'S CRYSTAL CAVE

You open your eyes groggily. Light flickers and flashes in mad patterns as if you had fallen into a giant kaleidoscope. Colours shimmer and dance, blending into delicate traceries and patterns. Your right cheek stings as if someone had been slapping it.

'Come on. Come on. No time to waste.'

A white-bearded old man is leaning over you, his pointed hat askew. Behind him, the dancing colours form a rainbow halo.

'What. . .?' you ask, stupidly.

'Come on, Pip,' the white-bearded man says crossly. 'Just pull yourself together. And don't

'Me Merlin,' he says

pretend you don't recognise me. You do. Or you will. Merlin. Got that? Merlin. Say, "Merlin".'

'Merlin. . .' you echo, frowning.

That's it – Merlin. Good. Fine. We're making progress. And you're Pip.' He points a bony finger at his chest. 'Me Merlin. You Pip.'

'Me Pip. You Merlin,' you repeat, feeling a bit of a fool. You sit up. You are in the strangest place you have ever seen: a vast cavern of pure crystal. Crystal stalagmites rise up from the floor. Crystal stalactites hang down from the roof. The walls are rough, unworked outcrops of crystal. The roof is crystal. The floor is crystal. You have been lying on a large, rectangular slab: that too is crystal. The cavern is well lit by torches – how many torches you could not begin to guess, for each one reflects and reflects again in the crystal, making it impossible to count. You turn your head slowly. Portions of the natural crystal have been worked and cut into shapes: there are crystal tables, crystal benches, even what looks suspiciously like a crystal throne on a crystal dais. Even the cabinets and chests are crystal, so their contents can be seen easily within them.

'Merlin?' you say again. 'Is it you?'

'Yes, yes,' Merlin mutters impatiently. 'Quite definitely me and in grave danger of having my pension docked. Dreadful business. Are you properly awake?'

You nod, dumbly, still three-quarter ways

entranced by your surroundings.

Merlin catches your look. 'My crystal cave,' he explains. 'Interesting, isn't it? Very few people have even been here, you know, except for me. Very few. I brought Atilla the Hun once, but he broke some of the furniture. So I don't do much entertaining here now. It's mainly used for magic. The crystal focuses earth energies, you know, and that makes magic easier. Now, are you properly awake?'

You nod again; properly awake or not, you are still quite confused.

'Well,' says Merlin, 'now you're here, I'd better tell you what the trouble is. A Brass Dragon. That's what the trouble is. Wiped out an entire monastery, monks and all. Probably deserved it, of course. Can't stand monks myself – always creeping around in cloisters instead of doing anything useful. But the Archbishop was annoyed and the King wants to keep on the right side of him, so my pension will be docked unless we do something about it. Unless *you* do something about it, that is, Pip. Definitely a job for a fighter this. Somebody who knows about getting rid of Brass Dragons. You do know about getting rid of them, don't you?'

You shake your head. 'No.'

'Never mind, you soon will. The trick with Brass Dragons is to kill them before they kill you. That's all there is to it really. Except for closing the Gateway, of course.'

'Gateway?' That was you again, thoroughly confused.

'Gateway,' Merlin says. 'You aren't one of these idiots who think Brass Dragons come from Hell, are you?'

'No,' you say warily; although in truth you haven't the faintest idea where Brass Dragons come from.

'Good,' says Merlin. 'Because they don't. They come from the Ghastly Kingdom of the Dead. Every one of them. Yes, indeed. Without exception. The Ghastly Kingdom of the Dead is what you might call their *natural habitat.* And a very nasty natural habitat it is; but that's a different story. So when you find a Brass Dragon wandering round Avalon – or anywhere else on Earth for that matter – it follows that one of the Gateways to the Ghastly Kingdom must be open. Otherwise the dragon couldn't have got out, could it? So we – you, that is – must kill the dragon, then close the Gateway. Nothing else for it. If we – you – leave the Gateway open, heaven knows what else might get out. Brass Dragons aren't the worst you'll find in the Ghastly Kingdom of the Dead: that's why they call it "ghastly". So off you go now and get this mess cleared up. I'll trot off to Camelot and tell the King that everything's in hand.'

'Just a minute!' you protest.

Merlin holds up one skinny hand. 'You're right. You're right. You need LIFE POINTS. Can't do much in my Time without them, can you? No, indeed. Right. Now, roll your dice. Two dice once, or one die twice. Doesn't matter which.'

You roll the dice while Merlin watches with a gimlet eye.

'Now add the scores together,' he tells you. 'You won't get less than 2 and you can't get more than 12. That's the way it is with LIFE POINTS. With your LIFE POINTS anyway. *Now multiply your answer by 4,*' Merlin says. 'That's your LIFE POINTS. Write them down. Quickly, now.'

He looks around him furtively, as if he might be worried somebody was listening, then leans forward and whispers something in your ear: 'If you don't think you have enough, do the whole thing again. You can do it three times, if you want, and pick the best score. But not more than three times. More than that interferes with the spell and we don't want that, do we? Not when my pension's at stake.'

Merlin straightens up and goes on much more loudly. 'Now, fighting. There's going to be a lot of fighting, I'm afraid. But at least it's not as painful as fighting in your own world. You just roll dice, for you and your opponent. Quite easy, really. Two dice each time. Look – I'll make it simple for you.'

'First, you roll dice to see who has the first strike. Roll for your opponent, then for yourself. Highest score gets first hit. You always do that unless surprise comes into it. And if it does, you'll be told at the time, so that's all right.'

'Next, you roll two dice each time a strike is made. If you're rolling for *your* strike, you have to roll a 6 or better, otherwise you've missed. When you're rolling for your opponent, you'll be told what he, she or it needs to hit you. If it isn't mentioned, take it that they need a 6 as well. Anything you roll *above* the strike figure counts as damage. Damage is subtracted from your (or your opponent's) LIFE POINTS.'

'That's how you fight. At least that's how it goes with a fist fight. If you're using weapons, you do more damage. If you're wearing armour, it cuts down on damage. And since you'll be using *this*, you'll generally only need a 4 or better to hit somebody. . .'

This turns out to be something rather interesting. Merlin takes a wooden case from beneath one of the crystal tables and opens it carefully. Inside is the most beautifully made little sword you have ever seen. . .

If you have read The Castle of Darkness turn to 1. If not, go to 2.

1

'EJ!' you gasp. 'You've kept EJ!'

'Hallo, Pip,' says Excalibur Junior, the talking sword which accompanied you on your adventure through *The Castle of Darkness* and played such a sterling part in doing down the wicked Wizard Ansalom.

EJ's reappearance is good news indeed, for it means you will only need to throw a 4 on two dice to hit an enemy, when you're using him. What's more, EJ scores an additional 5 points of damage above what the dice shows each time he strikes successfully. (The bad news is, of course, that he talks too much, but you're just going to have to put up with that as you did last time!)

While you're reminiscing with EJ, Merlin takes something else out of the box – the neat dragonskin jacket you wore in your last adventure: the one that subtracts 4 points from any damage scored against you. These are two very important items, Pip. They could mean the difference between life and death on an adventure.

Now go to **3**.

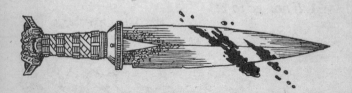

2

'Now this,' says Merlin, 'is Excalibur Junior. A very special sword. Made him myself, so I should know. He is an exact model of King Arthur's sword. An exact model, except smaller. And he talks – unlike King Arthur's Excalibur. Non-stop sometimes. Say hallo to Pip, EJ.'

To your amazement, the sword says dutifully, 'Hallo, Pip.'

In something akin to awe, you reach out and take hold of the sword. It feels beautifully balanced, light but powerful.

'Wow!' you remark, using an expression that isn't heard much in King Arthur's time.

But Merlin seems to understand it. 'Wow, indeed,' he says. 'When you use that sword, you only need to roll a 4 on two dice to hit somebody – it's part of the magic. And you score an additional 5 points of damage over and above any the dice may show. That's part of the magic, too.'

Now go to **4**.

3

If you have previously adventured through *The Castle of Darkness* you may have picked up some useful items there. You are allowed to bring these with you now, *but only if you actually found them in the Castle, and only if you still had them when you completed that adventure.* The following list will remind you about the items which were hidden in the Castle of Darkness. And *no cheating*, otherwise you'll break the spell!

1. *Luckstone.* This allows you to add, or subtract, 3 points to or from any dice roll you may make.

2. *Double-headed copper coin.* This is useful if you find yourself in a gambling game since it allows you to cheat like mad and win every toss. How many gambling games you're likely to get into in this adventure is quite another matter, but you never know. . .

3. *The Tinglering the Zombie wore.* So far nobody has quite figured out what a Tinglering actually does, but it certainly *seems* to be magic, so it may be worth taking.

4. *The Globule Wand from Ansalom's Laboratory.* This fires a luminous green glob which messes up an enemy so completely you can hit him four times before he gets a chance to hit back. Roll *one* die to find out how many globs are in the wand for the present adventure.

5. *The magic duck given you by the Poetic Fiend.* This little wooden duck will switch off any magic being used against you (or around you for that matter) so that, for example, a Fireball would fizzle out, or an invisible creature become visible. You can use the duck *once only* during any adventure.

6. *Scroll of Healing.* This is a spell which, when read aloud, will restore you to full LIFE POINTS. May be used *once only* during an adventure.

7. *Scroll of Teleportation*. This spell will take you back instantly to any Section you have previously visited. May be used *once only* during an adventure.

8. *Scroll of Death*. This spell will kill anything – including you! You read it and throw two dice. If you score a double 6, a double 3 or a double 1, you're dead. Score anything else and the spell kills your opponent, however powerful he, she or it may be.

NOTE: Items 6, 7 and 8 may only be taken if they were not used in the *Castle of Darkness*.

9. *Scroll of Hypnotism*. You must throw a 5 or better on two dice for this spell to work. If it does, your opponent will fall into a trance and you can safely ignore him. Does not work on dragons, unfortunately.

10. *Scroll of Poison Antidote*. Can be used to cure yourself of poisoning.

11. *The Crystal Ball in Ansalom's Laboratory* is now broken. You can take it with you if you like, but it won't work.

12. If you had any *Firefinger Bolts* or *Fireballs* remaining after your last adventure these may be added to the ones available to you through your spells in this adventure. They work a bit differently this time though, as you'll discover.

13. You may take up to 10 PERMANENT LIFE

points earned in *The Castle of Darkness* and add them to your total in this adventure.

Now go to **4**.

4

'Is that it?' you ask frowning.

'No,' says Merlin. 'No, indeed. Mustn't be impatient. Sometimes you'll find that a creature isn't as evil as it looks and that it doesn't want to fight you. To find out, roll one die once for your opponent and one die three times for yourself. If you score *less* than your enemy, he has given you a Friendly Reaction and you can continue on your way.

'If it all gets too much for you, you can try getting some LIFE POINTS back by *Sleeping* (you can do this any time except when actually in battle). It's not quite as simple as it sounds though. Roll one die. If you get a 1, 2, 3, or 4 you must turn to *Dreamtime* at the back of the book, where you might lose *even more* LIFE POINTS. If you get a 5 or 6 you have slept successfully and can get back two dice rolls' worth of LIFE POINTS. It's a bit of a gamble, really. But generally you'll be far too busy fighting to sleep. So you'll need your equipment and weapons – '

'And magic,' you say quickly, wondering what you are getting yourself into.

'– and magic. Won't get far against a Brass Dragon without magic. Right. Take this.' And from the depths of his robe (a powder-blue robe, not his usual white one) he pulls out a scroll, which he hands you.

You unroll the scroll which, like most of Merlin's scrolls, is written on excellent quality parchment, but marred by blots. Although you may have hoped it to be a *magical* scroll, it is not; however it does have your name on it.

You look up at Merlin, frowning. 'What's this?'

He seems embarrassed and does not meet your eye. 'Your shopping list. Just a few items you might need.'

'But why does it have the cost beside each one?'

Merlin coughs. 'I'm afraid you're going to have to buy your gear. Since the King docked my pension, I can't afford to equip you. So you'll have to buy your own.'

'But I don't have any money!' you protest.

'That is quite true,' Merlin agrees. 'And it might be a real problem if I hadn't foreseen it.' He opens a small crystal cabinet and takes from it two transparent cubes which, on closer inspection, you see to be dice. 'Magic dice,' he explains shortly. 'They convert enthusiasm into money. Can't use them myself since I haven't much enthusiasm left after the King docked my pension. But a young person like yourself should have lots of enthusiasm.' He hands you the dice. 'Throw them firmly on to the ground.'

Pip's Shopping List

Item	Cost (in Silver)
Backpack	1
Carpentry Hammer	1
Axe	1
Rope (15 m coil)	2
Torches (per doz)	1
Waterbag	1
Tent	10
Sack (per six)	½
Blanket	1
Lamp	2
Container of oil	1
Climbing spikes (per doz)	½
Fish-hooks (per doz)	½
Harp	5
Lute	4
Horn	3
Bandages (per 15m roll)	½
Knife	1
Tinderbox	½
Stakes (per doz)	½
Change of clothes	10
Change of boots	5
Parchment (per sheet)	½
Quill and powdered ink	1
Food pack (five days rations)	5
Cooking utensils	10
Healing Potion (1 doz)	3

There's nothing else for it but to throw the dice, Pip. As you do so, they explode in a silent flash of golden light. But just before the explosion, you could see the score. Roll your own dice to find out what it was. Every point scored represents a Gold Piece. And 1 Gold Piece is equal to 10 Silver Pieces. Looks as though you may be able to afford some equipment after all.

Merlin coughs again. 'Weapons too. And armour, if you want it.' He produces a second scroll. ''Fraid weapons and armour are quite expensive these days. . .'

Available Weapons and Armour	Damage	Cost (in Silver)
Battleaxe	+4	20
Dagger	+2	5
Flail	+2	5
War Hammer	+3	15
Lance	+5	40
Mace	+4	20
Sword	+3	20
Chainmail	−3	100
Leather	−2	50
Plate	−4	120

You look at the two parchment lists, then look at Merlin with a distinctly sinking feeling. This is going to be some costly mission. What you must now do, Pip, is spend your money wisely to equip yourself for the adventure to follow. Remember, all prices on the lists are given in *Silver* Pieces and there are 10 Silver Pieces to 1 Gold Piece.

Take a little time to decide what you might need. Obviously a weapon of some sort is a high priority for those times when EJ is unco-operative, or a different weapon is more suitable than a sword. You can't use more than one weapon at a time though. If your LIFE POINTS are low, it might be worthwhile investing in some armour, although it is very costly and buying some means you will have little or nothing left for other necessities. If you have adventured through *The Castle of Darkness* and have the magical dragonskin jacket, you can put armour on top and have *extra* protection.

Don't forget you may have to travel a long way to find this rampaging Brass Dragon, so a supply of food might be a good idea unless you plan to live off the land. But it's entirely up to you what you decide to buy: just so long as you have the gold to cover it. Write down the things you're taking on your Quest Journal and remember that if it isn't on your list during the adventure, then you can't use it. If you have any money left over, write that down too. Money can come in very handy on a long journey.

'Well now,' says Merlin, 'all set, look you, Bach?' (Lapsing into his native Welsh in his impatience to get you going so he can reclaim his pension.)

'I think so,' you say uncertainly. 'Except that I don't really know where to go. . .'

'Don't worry about that,' Merlin says. 'I've been following up that stupid monster on my crystal ball and I know where it's hiding out. Dragon Cavern. Quite obvious, really. Most of them hide out in Dragon Cavern between bouts of pillaging and so forth. The place is full of dragons of one sort and another. And maidens, of course. But only one Brass Dragon, which is the one you want, so don't waste your time hacking at the other dragons. Unless they attack you, which they probably will.'

'I don't know how to get to Dragon Cavern,' you protest.

'Not to worry,' Merlin says cheerfully. 'I'll draw you a map.'

'You said you'd teach me magic,' you say bluntly.

'Magic!' Merlin cries, striking his forehead a resounding blow. 'Yes, magic. Of course. Good thing for you I remembered. You won't last long in the Dragon Cavern without a bit of magic.'

Stumbling on the hem of his powder-blue robe, he half runs (in his impatience) to a crystal bookshelf from which he takes down a huge, leather bound tome entitled

MAGIC FOR BEGINNERS

He begins to thumb through it hurriedly. 'Sit still,' he says. 'Don't fidget. Got something to write with? Good. Then write this down:

RULES OF MAGIC

Rule 1. Every spell you try to cast will cost you 3 LIFE POINTS *whether it works or not!*

Rule 2. No spell can be thrown more than *three times* in any adventure. Once thrown, it is used up whether successful or not.

Rule 3. No spell works at all unless you score 7 or more with a throw of two dice.

You nod, busily writing down the Rules of Magic. They seem simple enough, except for one thing. 'But I don't know any spells,' you say.

'Of course you don't! Wouldn't have to learn them if you did. I'm going to give you a book of spells. Not this one, don't worry – too heavy to carry. A little one that will fit into your backpack. Just a few spells, a very few spells, but well chosen. You can have a quick look through it before you start off, if you like.'

Pip's First Spell Book

Spell	Effect
Pip's Armour of Nearly Impenetrable Coruscation (P.A.N.I.C. for short)	Throws a shimmering, spinning wall of light around the user. This light acts exactly like plate armour, subtracting 4 points from any damage scored against the user. What's more, this effect is *additional* to any deductions made for actual armour, dragonskin jacket etc.
Pip's Outlandish Wallop (P.O.W. for short)	Adds +10 to the damage caused by the next blow delivered by the user. This is additional to damage shown by dice and weapon damage.

Spell	Effect

Pip's Instant Levity and Laughter
(P.I.L.L. for short)

Causes the user's opponent to fall about laughing so heartily that he/she/it misses three consecutive turns during combat.

Pip's Attacking Dart
(P.A.D. for short)

Allows user to launch a magical dart against an enemy out of combat range. The dart never misses provided the spell is properly cast and causes 10 damage points. An enemy so attacked cannot immediately strike back unless he has some long-distance weapon such as a bow or spear.

Pip's Immunity to Poison
(P.I.P. for short, oddly enough)

If cast *before* poison is taken, the spell renders the user immune to its effects whatever results are shown by the dice. The spell DOES NOT WORK if cast *after* the poison is taken. It comes in useful when the user wishes to sample some unknown substance that might be dangerous.

Pip's Instant Neutraliser
(P.I.N. for short)

The use of this spell counteracts the effect of one (only) spell placed on an *object* (not a person or living creature). It is useful for opening magically locked chests, doors etc.

Pip's Immense Rapid Repeater
(Pi R Squared, for short)

During combat, the spell enables the user to move twice as fast as usual, enabling him/her to get in TWO blows in succession each time his/her turn comes round throughout a given combat.

Very Special Spell
INVISIBILITY
(I.N.V.I.S.I.B.I.L.I.T.Y. for short)

This very special spell may only be used ONCE per adventure at a cost of 15 LIFE POINTS . . . and even then only in certain sections of the adventure. (The sections where Invisibility is possible are labelled as such, so don't waste LIFE POINTS trying it anywhere else.) The effect of the spell is to render the user totally invisible

Firefinger

This causes a bolt of lightning to emerge from your finger and zap 10 LIFE POINTS from an enemy. This spell gives you ten Firefinger Bolts in all. Once cast successfully, the spell may not be used again.

Spell	Effect
Fireball	Creates a giant fireball in the palm of your hand which you can then hurl at an enemy to cause him 75 points of damage. This spell gives you only *two* Fireballs, one for each hand. Once cast successfully, the spell may not be used again.*

*But you can keep any Lightning Bolt or Fireball you don't use right away and use it later.

EXTREMELY IMPORTANT NOTE:

Except for INVISIBILITY, any spell you have can be used in *any* section of your adventure. It is up to you to keep a note on your Quest Journal of what spells you have used up and what spells you still carry.

It is also up to you to remember to use them!

'That's it,' says Merlin. 'That's your magic. That's your spells. You can use each one three times only. Unless you find another copy, of course. That sometimes happens during an adventure, so keep your eyes peeled. Not much to magic, really, so long as you remember the basic rule. *Never use a spell when you're nearly dead, otherwise the loss of LIFE POINTS will kill you.* Make your roll to find out if the spell worked. If it didn't, it didn't and there's nothing you can do about it, unless you want to try again. But not more than three times. A spell thrown is used whether it works or not. Precious things, spells. That's why you don't find many Wizards about. It's a very frustrating profession, fraught with all sorts of trials, tribulations and dangers—like getting your pension docked.

'You're nearly ready to leave now, Pip. But first I must tell you about Experience. Every time you fight a battle or solve a puzzle you will gain 1 EXPERIENCE POINT. 20 of these make 1 PERMANENT LIFE POINT which can be added to your existing LIFE POINTS – even if this brings them higher than they were to start with. You can take up to 10 PERMANENT LIFE POINTS into future adventures and add them to the LIFE POINTS you roll up.'

And here he withdraws a parchment scroll (stained with age or possibly tea and displaying the familar blots) from the sleeve of his robe.

'Finally,' he says. 'Your map. This is a copy of a

very rare and ancient map which I made myself. The copy, that is, not the ancient map. Don't lose it, otherwise you won't know where to go, will you? It shows you how to get to Dragon Cavern. Not many people know how to get there. In fact, I think I may be the only one. But now you'll know the secret too. Prepare for your trip carefully, so far as you can afford to. Then follow the map. Once you're in Dragon Cavern, I'm afraid you'll have to fend for yourself. Nobody's ever managed to map it, so you'll have to make your own way once you're in there. But use this map to *get* you there. Off you go, now.'

And Merlin, who (for all his bumbling and foolishness) is still the greatest Wizard in Avalon, waves his arms in a magical gesture. Slowly, but with an awesome inevitability, both he and the crystal cave begin to fade completely away . . .

Something is nudging you in the back, Pip. You turn and find yourself staring into the soulful brown eyes of Wandering Wanda, your favourite cow in the small herd now owned by your adopted parents, Freeman John and Goodwife Mary. And if this is a Wandering Wanda, then the pasture in which you are now standing must be the back field of the farm on which you live. How on earth did you get here? Only Merlin could say. But as you glance down at your feet, you find the various items of equipment you decided to spend your gold on in the crystal cave. More to the point, clasped in your hot little hand is a tea-stained scroll on which has been drawn a map.

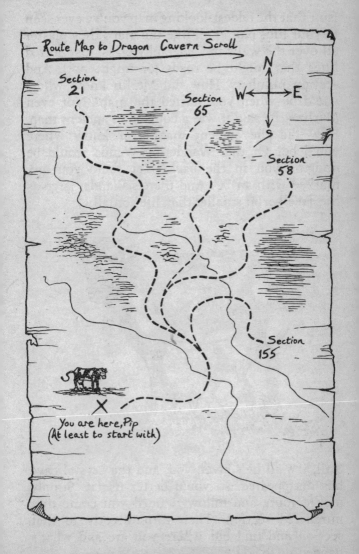

Isn't that the oddest-looking map you've ever seen
in your life? Not at all like the maps they plaster
all over the walls in Geography class. Just dotted
lines that might be roads (or might not). And
section numbers. How did Merlin know where
you'd be when you started the map? Not even
Merlin – he said it was a copy of an ancient map.
How did the ancient mapmaker know where
you'd be? Or that Wandering Wanda would be
nudging you in the back? Yet there you are,
marked with an 'X'. And there's Wanda, large as
life. (Well, a bit smaller than life actually.)

Still, it's all he's given you, and the crystal cave
has disappeared, so you'd better use it. Simply
pick a route and follow it until you come to a
numbered section. Then turn directly to that
section and find out where you are and what's
happening to you.

Don't forget to take your equipment and weapons. (And spells!) You'll notice that the entrance to Dragon Cavern isn't actually marked. Perhaps because it's secret. But it must be there somewhere, maybe in one of those sections. You're just going to have to travel and find out, Pip. Because wherever it is . . .

The Adventure begins!

THE
ADVENTURE

5

The wood seems to close around you as you enter,
and after only moments the path peters out,
leaving you to hack your way through shrub,
scrub and undergrowth as best you can. The going
gets more and more difficult, more and more
confusing, until you realise you are thoroughly
lost. You stand for a moment, scratching your
head. When this does nothing to help your
situation, you make the only decision possible.
Roll two dice to find out if there's any way out of
here.

Score 2 – 6 and go to **31**.
Score 7 – 12 and go to **17**.

6

It's fanged you in the kneecap! Savage little beast leaped up and sank its filthy chompers right in to the bone! The pain is only cruel. If you plan to fight this thing, deduct 2 from every dice throw you make on account of your gammy leg.

The White Rabbit has 25 LIFE POINTS and fangs with +3 damage. It requires only a 5 or better to strike so long as it attacks below a metre in height (which it will: it's not stupid).

If you want to run, go to **5**.
If you fight and the White Rabbit kills you, go to **14**.
If you fight and kill the White Rabbit you have the option of returning to **65** and reconsidering your options; or returning to **11** (where you will undoubtedly find a *second* White Rabbit) and reconsidering your options there.

NOTE: If at any stage in the fight the White Rabbit gets three successful strikes against you in a row, go to **26**.

7

If you decide to use your axe to cut down a tree which might form a bridge across the chasm, go to **35**.
If you decide to use rope or spikes to help you climb down that sheer cliff face, go to **27**.

8

Still lost in the fog, Pip. Wander about until you reach **42**.

9

You seem to have walked for miles, with the village still in sight but no nearer. Now you are exhausted and hungry, so you decide to rest and eat some of your rations. You leave the track and sit on the grass, your back against a tree stump near a little copse. There is a clear stream nearby where you can drink. The village remains in sight, no nearer and no further.

As you open your pack, a voice behind you says, 'Good morrow, Your Honour.'

You spring up, hand reaching for your sword, then hesitate. A tiny little man, dressed in brown and green, has emerged from the copse and is looking at you with dark, twinkling eyes. He does not carry arms and certainly does not seem very dangerous.

'That's a fine-looking bit of grub you have there, Your Honour,' says the little man. 'A morsel or two would go down well with a fella who hasn't eaten in a week.'

Do you offer to share your rations with the tiny trencherman? If so, go to **36**.
Do you point out politely that you have a long way to go and will need the food for yourself? If so, go to **22**.

10

A blink. A flicker. You are in the village, Pip. No doubt about that. Right there, without walking another step. How strange. It's a pretty village; small but pretty. Thatched cottages . . . a village green . . . a picturesque little stone-built church. And not a soul about. Not a *living* soul.

You are standing on a patch of beaten earth, a little rutted and muddy as if it was used fairly often. There is a long building to the north-east of you, and due east the oddest garden you have ever seen – all the plants seem to be made from stone and there are statues of monsters dotted through it. Beyond the garden are cottages and beyond the cottages you can see the church spire. The entire village is enclosed by a stout wooden stockade, very sturdily built and, by the looks of it, extremely difficult to climb. To the south-east are more cottages and a high stone wall.

Turn to the map of the village at the front of the book, Pip. You are free to explore as you wish. Go anywhere, see anything. The buildings and a few other places are all numbered, so you'll know which Section to turn to as you explore each one.

Oh, one more thing, Pip . . . Have you noticed there isn't any way out?

11

You've reached a clearing. Well, it's better than hacking your way through the undergrowth, even though there isn't much to see here. The clearing itself is roughly circular and about five, maybe six, metres in radius, with a large oak tree growing in the middle and a Rabbit sitting on a little hillock eyeing you suspiciously from near its rabbit hole. And that's about it, apart from a few bluebells.

So what do you do now, Pip? Sit under the tree and have a little think? Wait a minute! That's a white Rabbit. A *white* Rabbit! You know, a White Rabbit, same as in *Alice in Wonderland*! It couldn't be *that* sort of White Rabbit, could it? Yes, it could, you know. It really could! This is a magical adventure and you can't get more magical than a White Rabbit, can you? Maybe that rabbit hole is the entrance to Wonderland. Maybe the Ghastly Kingdom of the Dead is just another name for Wonderland! Well, it *could* be. So what are you going to do, Pip?

If you want to try chatting up the Rabbit, go to **6**.
If you want to sit under the tree for a little think, go to **46**.

12
Yip, Pip, magic should work OK, providing you manage it properly. Go to **23**.

13
What's this? It might be a heat haze, except the weather isn't all that hot. And a heat haze doesn't behave like that.

It's a shimmer in the air ahead of you. But a shimmer with clear edges, two metres high, more than a metre wide. It looks like a doorway. A

13 Through the shimmering doorway is a village

shimmering doorway. Beyond it stands the village, distant as ever.

Will you enter the shimmering doorway? If so, go to **10**.
Will you carefully walk round the doorway? If so, go to **33**.

14

You open your eyes slowly. Somewhere in the background, a hidden orchestra is playing the Funeral March from *Saul*. Around you is the crystal cave. Standing over you, looking extremely cross, is Merlin.

'Gone and gotten yourself killed, haven't you?' he snaps. 'Very careless. Well, you'll just have to start again, won't you. And do a bit better this time, otherwise I'll never get my pension back. Just you roll dice the way I showed you to get yourself some money, then use it to buy more

equipment and so on from the lists. Then turn back to your map and start again from the spot marked 'x'.

With which he wanders off into the depths of the cave, mumbling something into his beard about young people these days . . .

15

Your chosen approach is no good in these circumstances. Return to the Section you've just come from and pick another option, but lose the incentive so your enemy gets in the first strike.

16

You trudge onwards, soon leaving the dark forest far behind. The scenery is more cheerful now, but after a time the route dips and enters a valley. As you continue, you find yourself entering an ever thickening mist. Soon the mist becomes a fog. And soon you can hardly see your nose in front of your face. Your sense of direction, normally so keen, is weakening, fading, disappearing altogether.

Oh, blast, Pip – you're lost! Nothing else for it but to roll two dice to decide which way to go.

Score 2 – 4 and go to **5**.
Score 5 – 7 and go to **8**.
Score 8 – 12 and go to **64**.

17

Sorry, you still seem to be completely lost. Roll dice again.

Score 2 – 6 and go to **73**.
Score 7 – 12 and go to **82**.

18

Well, here goes! You gather up your equipment and move back along the track to give yourself the longest possible run. You take a deep breath, touch wood (there's lots of it about in the forest) and thunder off at top speed towards the chasm. Roll two dice to see if you make it safely over. (And good luck.)

Roll 2 to 6 and go to **14**.
Roll 7 to 12 and go to **85**.

19

Someone is walking towards you on the roadway. Someone BIG. He walks funny too, rolling a bit from side to side as if he was having just a little difficulty keeping his balance. He must weigh a ton – the ground is shaking as he approaches. And he's a weird colour: all sort of slate grey.

Don't like the look of this, Pip, not one bit. He's walking straight at you. Good grief, it isn't a man at all. It's . . . it's . . . it's a *statue*! A walking statue! A Stone Man! And he's carrying a stone sword!

'Now just a minute –' you call as the Stone Man

19 The Stone Man lumbers towards you

continues to clump down on you. But it's no good. He begins to swing his sword.

This is a fight, Pip, and no mistake. No avoiding it either, however peace-loving you might be. It's kill or be killed here. But will your weapons be effective against a *Stone* Man? Only one way to find out.

Do you try to fight him with weapons? If so, go to **15**.
Do you decide to use magic? If so, go to **12**.
If you decide to use a magical weapon (like EJ), go to **32**.

20

Phew, what a pong! These are stables by the smell of them, although it looks as though they haven't been used in years. The stalls are broken down and the hay rotting. Pieces of leather harness hang from nails in the walls, looking as if they'd fall apart if you tried to put them on a horse. Fortunately you don't have to, as there are no horses here.

If you want to spend a little time searching, go to **71**.
If not, return to your map and decide where to explore next.

21

The forest flanks you on each side as you follow your route north-east. The trees are as densely packed and gloomily threatening as ever, but at least the path ahead seems clear and free of obstacles. Until, that is, you reach a chasm that cuts directly across it. Mmmm.

You walk to the edge. The chasm drops down in a sheer cliff face for almost sixty metres. At the bottom is a turbulent, fast-flowing river. You look across and note your path continues on the other side. The distance across you would estimate at no more than five or six metres. You just *might* be able to jump across if you took a long enough run. As against that, you're tired and carrying a heavy load of equipment. Mmmm. Let's check what you've got with you.

If you're carrying a rope, climbing spikes or axe (or a battleaxe) among your armaments go to **7**.
If you decide to try jumping across, go to **18**.
If you think there might be a way across by entering the forest again, go to **5**.

22

'Sure don't I understand that perfectly well,' says the little man, not at all offended or put out. 'You just sit there and piggy away at your fine meal, and I'll sit on the stump and keep you company for a bit.'

As you eat, it occurs to you that the little man might know something about the mystery of the village, so you ask him for directions.

'That place yonder?' he asks. 'Sure, don't I know it

well, having been there on many an occasion meself and met up with some of the finest, kindest and most helpful people in the whole of Avalon. Stonemarten Village they call it.'

'I've been walking towards it for hours and don't seem to be getting any nearer,' you tell him.

'Aye, it's a hard one to reach all right,' he agrees. 'But if you take my advice, you'll try **29**.'

If you take his advice, go to **29**.
If you prefer to make your own way unaided, go to **19**.

23

The Stone Man has 28 LIFE POINTS. He's a bit slow on his feet and so needs to roll an 8 or better to hit you with his stone sword. As against that, the sword will cause +4 damage if it gets you. Good luck.

If the Stone Man kills you, go to **14**.
If you kill the Stone Man, go to **37**.

24

This is like no church you've ever been in, Pip. At least it is, but it isn't. There's an aisle and pews and an altar and an organ and a pulpit and a lectern and all the rest, right down to the stained-glass windows. But the whole kit and caboodle is covered thick with dust and cobwebs. They're everywhere. They brush against your face as you move, and the dust rises in little clouds from under your feet.

This does not look like a very religious community, Pip. You step forward and . . .

Da-da-da-boom!

That's an organ! The church organ has started to play! You start, and swing round at the sound. Your eyes sweep upwards towards the organ loft, but the cobwebs obscure your view.

'Ah ha ha ha ha ha ha!'

Maniac laughter! It echoes throughout the entire building as the organ music stops abruptly. You drop your hand involuntarily to your sword hilt, which is just as well, because swinging from a rope high above you is a cloaked and masked figure carrying a glittering blade.

'Beware!' it screams as it lands only a few metres in front of you. 'Beware the Phantom of the Village Church!' With which it lunges at you viciously with its sword.

This is definitely a fight, Pip, whatever you may think. The Phantom has 30 LIFE POINTS but wears no armour, so you score full damage each time you hit. As against that, it's good with the sword, so it only needs to roll a 5 or better to hit you. Its sword does + 3 damage.

If the Phantom kills you, go to **14**.
If you kill the Phantom, go to **87**.

25

You emerge into a volcanic wasteland. All around you are lava flats, vast stretches of stone distorted into grotesque shapes, a rippled, pitted surface that is difficult to travel over. You are surrounded by high cliffs, their sheer faces towering upwards to vast heights. Let's hope you don't have to climb these, Pip: even with equipment it could take you the best part of a year.

It is gloomy here: the cliffs are so high they cut out much of the sunlight. It should be chill as well, but in fact the place is almost tropical, probably on account of some low-level volcanic activity. Certainly there is a sharp, acrid smell of sulphur, as if you had stepped into the very mouth of Hell.

You make your way forward carefully, ears straining for any sound. The ground is generally firm enough, although it crumbles slightly in places; and from time to time a low, almost sub-sonic rumbling shivers from below your feet, setting your nerves even more on edge. There are only two routes open to you – due north and north-east. All other directions are cut off either by the cliff faces or towering, tortured, twisted spires of rock.

If you decide to go north, turn to **62**.
If you decide to go north-east, turn to **84**.

25 You emerge into a volcanic wasteland

26

You've just been poisoned. That vicious little brute has poisoned fangs. What a mess this is. Throw two dice fast.

Score 2 – 4 and go to the dreaded **14**.
Score 5 – 8 and you're naturally immune to the poison. Return to **6** and continue fighting.
Score 9 and the White Rabbit has died from a massive allergic reaction from biting you too often. Go to **6** and read what to do now you've killed the Rabbit.
Score 10 – 12 and you've lost half your current LIFE POINTS and fallen unconscious. When you come to, the White Rabbit has somehow dragged you into the wood and disappeared. Go to **5**.

27

Right then, Pip, let's find out if you made that difficult climb. It's a very sheer face and even with ropes or spikes it's tricky. In fact, it's so tricky you might have second thoughts. If so, you can go back to **7** right now and reconsider your options. But if you decide to go ahead, roll two dice.

Score 2 – 8 and go to **49**.
Score 9 – 12 and go to **59**.

28

Stone leeks and lettuces, stone cabbages, stone peas, stone carrots, stone spinach, even stone potatoes. And over there you can clearly see stone flowers – roses, hyacinths, rhododendrons, lily of the valley, bachelor's buttons, buttercups and daisies. There must be an awful lot of lime in the soil here.

Those monster statues don't look too pleasant, Pip. Huge great fanged things with hairy chests and claws. Very nasty. And very lifelike. You would almost expect one of them to move at any second. In fact, that one over there actually *seemed* to move. A trick of the light, no doubt.

The ground isn't stone. It's ordinary soil, just like a normal garden. Except it's growing stone plants. What a weird place. Why should anybody want to grow stone plants, then set the whole garden through with lifelike statues of monsters? Are you sure that one didn't really move? No, of course it didn't.

You tug experimentally on a stone cauliflower and up it comes, roots and all. Stone roots, of course. What a very weird place. Have you noticed how cold it's become?

That monster DID move! It's turning towards you, all hairy chest and fangs!

Like a stroke of lightning you go for your sword, except your arm won't move! Run, Pip! Run! Your legs won't move either! You feel so cold. So very, very cold. The monster is walking towards you on great flat stone feet. You can't move a muscle and you're cold! Desperately you try to chant a spell, but even your lips and tongue won't move.

You're turning to stone, Pip! That's what it is.
That's definitely what it is! The monster is only a
few metres away now. It opens its great fanged
mouth.

At least you can still roll dice, Pip. Roll two now
to find out if you can get out of this mess.

Score 2 – 6 and go to **67**.
Score 7 – 10 and go to **70**.
Score 11 or 12 and go to **75**.

29

This can't be happening, Pip, but it has! You
followed his directions to the letter . . . and now
you're right back at the start, with Wandering
Wanda staring at you in amazement.

Nothing else for it, Pip, but to get your map and
start again. Still, you know a bit of the way now
and you may have learned to avoid some of the
worst dangers.

30

Looks like the remains of a stone watchtower,
Pip; and very, very old. In ruins now, of course.
Most of the tower itself has fallen in and the

whole area is covered with fallen stones and rubble. You could mess about here forever, spraining your ankle on loose stones. Why not just roll a couple of dice to see what, if anything, might happen to a worthy adventurer in this place?

Score 2 – 6 and go to **80**.
Score 7 – 12 and go to **88**.

31

Nope, still lost. Throw your dice again.

Score 2 – 6 and go to **17**.
Score 7 – 12 and go to **73**.

32

Not a bad choice, Pip. Magical weapons are effective here, although you will have to subtract 4 from any damage they cause.

Go to **23**.

33

The village vanishes and the road stretches endlessly before you. You turn, but the Shimmering Doorway is no longer there. There can be no question of turning back now. Nothing else for it but to press on.

Walk until your legs ache and the sun sets. Camp for the night where you can, then wake up to a fresh new day (it's raining – wouldn't you know) and go to **125**.

34

Why would anybody in their right mind want to explore this place? It's a graveyard, Pip. You knew it was a graveyard – you could see that quite plainly before you decided to come here! What on earth do you expect to find in a graveyard?

Well, what you have found is graves. And tombstones. And . . . Oh dear, it looks as if you've done it again, Pip: that grave over there is *open*! As you watch, a hand reaches up out of it and scrabbles at loose earth by the graveside!

Rush to **91** before the Thing gets you!

35

Roll two dice.

Score 2 – 6 and there just wasn't a suitable tree near enough. Go to **21** and reconsider your options.

Score 7 – 12 and go to **85**.

36

'That's mighty civil of you, Your Honour,' says the little man. 'I don't mind if I do, now you mention it.' And he climbs up on the stump to make himself comfortable.

As he eats (and he eats very heartily for someone of his size) he eyes you, your clothes and your weapons. 'Would I be right in supposing,' he says eventually, 'that you're a traveller or an adventurer?'

You nod.

'Didn't I think so by the look of you. You're not on your way to Dragon Cavern, by any chance?'

Will you tell him where you're headed? If so, go to **56**.
Will you keep your business to yourself? If so go to **22**.

37

Wow, was that some fight! For a while there it didn't look as though you were going to come through. Just shows what skill, courage and determination can do. You take a little time to recover, then walk further along your chosen route until you reach **13**.

38

It looks like a cottage, much like every other cottage. Whitewashed walls. Thatched roof. It's set against the stockade, of course, but so are several other cottages as, doubtless, you've noticed. Nonetheless you go in, since you've come this far. And since the door is ajar, going in presents no problem.

The cottage is deserted. Clean and tidy enough inside, but with that funny musty smell that lets you know nobody has lived here for years. But somebody did live here once. There are a few pieces of furniture around the place, ornaments on the mantle and pictures (scenic views) on the walls. *And there's a back door!* If there's a back door, it must mean there's a way out through the stockade!

If you want to go through the back door, turn to **92**.

If you'd rather stick around for a while, return to your map of Stonemarten Village and explore somewhere else.

39

As you approach this cottage you notice by the front door one of those ghastly plastic garden gnomes that are going to become extremely popular in a few centuries' time. Wait a minute! A plastic gnome in the days of King Arthur? Something badly wrong here, Pip.

'Hello, human person,' the Gnome says, as you stand staring at him in amazement.

'You're real?' you ask, stupidly.

'I think so,' says the Gnome. 'What can I do for you?'

Which is a very good question since all you'd really planned to do was nose around in his cottage and you can't very well tell him that. Eventually you say, 'I wonder, Gnoble Gnome, if by chance you know the best way to the Dragon's Cavern? Or indeed, any way out of this village might do.'

He gnods his gnomish head seriously. 'Of all the questions you might have asked, I have answers of a sort for those two. Have you money to pay for them?'

Pay for what?' you ask.

'The answers!' roars the Gnome peevishly. 'You don't think I'd part with valuable information for free, do you?'

'Of course not,' you lie through your teeth. 'How much do the answers cost?'

'That depends,' says the Gnome, a little more calmly now. 'I'm by way of being a sporting gnome, you see, so I'm quite prepared to let chance decide the price.'

With which he produces two dice from his pocket, very similar indeed to the dice you yourself are using. 'Would you care to examine these?' he asks. 'To ensure they are not loaded or interfered with in any way?'

You do so. This may be the Age of Chivalry, but chivalry doesn't extend to letting yourself get ripped off by a gnome. The dice, however, are perfectly normal.

'Now,' says the Gnome, 'you wish to know the way to Dragon Cavern. We'll make that Question 1. And you wish to know a way out of the village. We'll make that Question 2. Now we'll roll these perfectly normal dice and find out, in Gold Pieces, what each question is worth. For every point shown by the dice, the value will be 10 Gold Pieces. So you may get your question answered for as little as 20, or you may have to pay as much as 120.'

Write the dice score, multiplied by ten, in the spaces below:

Question 1:

Question 2:

Can you afford to pay to have your questions answered? Check your available money and valuables.

If you don't want to pay, whether you can afford to or not, return to your map and explore somewhere else – the Gnome won't mind (and you can always come back to the Section later, if you wish and have the money).

If you pay for an answer to Question 1, go to **93**.

If you pay for an answer to Question 2, go to **113**.

If you pay for both answers, pick either **93** or **113**.

40

Now that's better! A table ladened with jam tarts, trifle, apple pies, cakes, buns, bombes, tortes and goodies of every description. There's even a pitcher of home-made lemonade. And not a soul in sight! Tuck in, Pip. You need to fortify yourself when you can in a place like this!

Then go to **100**.

41

I say, Pip: what's bright green with purple teeth, stands upright on two legs and carries a dagger in

41 The creature eyes you hungrily

each hand? No, I don't know either, but there's one of them in this cottage. It's got 15 LIFE POINTS as well and it's looking at you hungrily.

I don't suppose you brought any spare rations, did you? If you've only got one food pack, it's no good offering that since you'll only starve later. But if you have a spare pack, the thing should have such indigestion by the time it's finished that it won't trouble you again. If you don't have any spare rations, you're into another fight, I'm afraid.

If you win, you can keep the daggers and the 10 Silver Pieces you'll find in the thing's pouch. (Could it be a sort of green and purple dagger-carrying kangaroo, do you think? Or a magic platypus? Or a very old wallaby? Or an Australian cricketer in fancy dress? We'll never know . . . You can also return to your map of the village and explore somewhere else. If you lose, it's back to **14**.

42

You're never going to believe this, Pip. There's bright sunshine everywhere and Wandering Wanda is nudging you in the back, looking stupid.

You've somehow come full circle and reached the place you started out from. Better check the map Merlin gave you and try again! You can pick any of the Sections shown to start out again.

43

Now we're getting somewhere! This cottage has a back door!

If you decide to go through the back door, turn to **92**.

If you decide not to, return to your map and continue exploring.

44

You enter the cottage and fall down a trap. Sorry to put it so bluntly, Pip, but you need to know right away when you're in trouble. And you may be in a lot of trouble.

First off, there are spikes in the bottom of the pit. Roll two dice to find out if any of them skewered you. Score 2–6 and at least one did. Score 7–12 and they missed you.

If you got skewered, roll your dice again to find the damage to your LIFE POINTS. If this kills you, go to **14**.

If you got skewered, there's more bad news – the spikes are poisoned. Roll two dice again to see if you're naturally immune. Score 2–6 and the poison does you no more harm. Score 7–12 and it's lethal: go to **14**.

Even if you missed the spikes, there's still the

problem of getting out. If you brought climbing equipment like spikes and rope, you can climb out fairly easily. Go to your map and explore another area of the village.

If you don't have the necessary equipment you're stuck there until you starve to death. Go to **14**.

45

How strange. It looks like a cottage. It's the shape of a cottage and the size of a cottage. But now you're close up you can see it isn't a cottage – it's a huge stone block with thatch on top. You spend ages trying to figure this one out, but eventually return to your map and explore another area of the village.

46

'Hallo, little person,' a deep, but curiously rustling voice says from somewhere up above you.

You look up into the branches of the tree, but there is no one to be seen.

'Of course there isn't,' the voice says clearly. 'Or rather there is. You're looking at me.'

'But I don't see you,' you protest.

'Yes, you do.'

'You mean . . . you're the tree? A talking tree?'

'Not just any old ordinary tree,' the voice says. 'I'm a Druid Oak. Very special sort of tree, that.

46 'I'm a Druid Oak,' the voice says

Keep clear of the Rabbit, incidentally: it's got poisonous teeth.'

'Thank you for the warning,' you say politely, even though you're completely bemused from talking to a tree (or at least from talking to a tree that answers back). 'I don't suppose you'd happen to know the way out of this wood, by any chance?'

'Of course. I've lived here a hundred years, haven't I?' And one thick branch moves, as if blown by a high wind, and points north-east.

If you decide to trust the tree, go to **77**.
If not, return to **11** and reconsider your options.

47

Count Dracula used to say that when you'd seen one crypt you'd seen them all. But whatever about that, this really does seem to be a rather special sort of crypt. For a start it's all done up in *pink* marble. And then again there's a brass plaque on the heavy wooden doorway which bears the words:

> *Oh footsore and weary traveller*
> *With dust on your feet and quite possibly*
> *Nits in your hair:*
> *Enter here and rest awhile*
> *And with fine poetry you I will beguile*
> *So push the door, my traveller fair*
> *And partake of my hospitably.*

Hospitably? Maybe he meant 'hospitality' but couldn't get that to rhyme with 'possibly'. Not that 'hospitably' rhymes very well with 'possibly', either.

Only one creature in the universe could write rhymes as badly as that. His fame is so widespread almost everybody in Avalon has heard of him at some time or another. Could it be . . .? Yes, it is! Below the plaque is an iron plate bearing the words:

THE CRYPT OF THE FIEND
(Please Knock)

Don't waste another moment, Pip! This will certainly be dangerous, but it should be well worthwhile. Go in! Go in!

If you decide to enter the Crypt of the Fiend, go to **107**.
If not, return to your map and explore some other part of the village.

48

You enter the cottage and the entire place caves in on top of you. It's no fun being an adventurer sometimes, Pip.

Go to **14**.

49

You cling precariously to the cliff face and edge your way downwards, searching for almost non-existent toeholds. In the chasm there is a strong cross wind which increases alarmingly as you descend. Now you've actually started, the whole

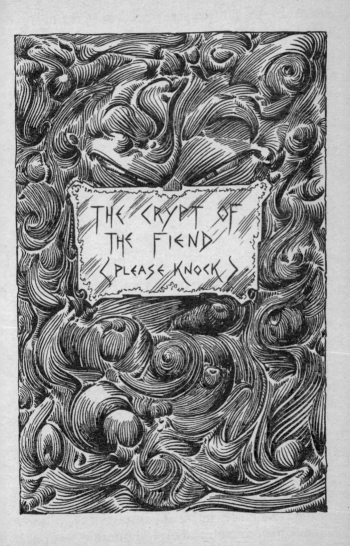

THE CRYPT OF
THE FIEND
(PLEASE KNOCK)

chasm looks far deeper than you previously imagined. Far deeper . . .

Don't look down!

It goes down for miles and miles and miles and miles and . . .

Don't look down!

and miles and miles and . . . dizzy . . .

You fall!

Go to **14**.

Snaarl!

What a nasty noise to hear as you open a cottage door, Pip. It's dark inside, so that for a moment all you can see is the glint of a pair of savage red eyes. Then the Wolf leaps from the cottage at your throat! It is huge – 31 LIFE POINTS – and does +3 damage with its fangs. It also has the first strike, by reason of surprise. Furthermore, its matted hide acts to some extent like armour, subtracting 1 point from any damage scored against it. Get the dice rolling, Pip ¬ this is another fight.

If the Wolf kills you, go to **14**.
If you kill the Wolf, you'll find a casket with 100 Gold Pieces inside the cottage. Take it, go back to your map and explore another section of the village.

51

If you weren't such a thorough sort of adventurer, Pip, you would have thought this was just a deserted old cottage. Nobody here, nothing of value, a few sticks of broken-down furniture . . . Just the sort of place where you'd turn right round and walk out again. Except you didn't, did you? You felt along the walls and over by the fireplace you found a funny little knob. When you twisted the funny little knob, a funny little secret door opened up in the wall, leading into a funny little secret passage.

Of course you don't *have* to explore the secret passage. You can simply return to your map of the village and explore some other area. But if you *do* want to explore the secret passage, it leads to **90**.

52

Somebody likes pot plants.

As you enter this cottage, your mind immediately conjures up pictures of a sweet little old lady pottering about in the peace and quiet of her rural home. The place is absolutely chock-a-block with plants. Ferns ... palms ... rubber plants ... bonsai trees ... creepers. Lots of creepers. There are creepers all over the place. The creepers are *moving*! They are wrapping themselves around you, Pip! Roll two dice to see if you can get your sword arm free.

Score 2 – 6 and you're firmly held. Unable to fight, you will be slowly strangled and digested by the creepers. Spare yourself unnecessary suffering by going at once to **14**.

Score 7 – 12 and you get your sword out. Once you have a sword, it's no contest. You hack those nasty creepers into tiny little pieces with no damage whatsoever to yourself. That will teach them! Now return to your map and explore another part of the village.

53

Fine adventurer you turned out to be! Can't even find your way out of ... oh, never mind! Just roll your dice again. And try to do it right this time!

Score 2 – 6 and go to **73**.
Score 7 – 12 and go to **17**.

54

Big building. When you enter, you find it's a grain store. But like almost everything else in this crummy village, the grain smells pretty musty.

If you think there's nothing of interest here, return to your map and explore some other section of the village.
If you want to explore the store thoroughly, go to **104**.

55

'Halt, Varlet! Darest thou disturb my meditations!'

It's not what you might expect to hear on entering a country cottage, but it's what you do hear on entering this one. And the words come from a figure clad head to toe in jet-black armour. Could this be the notorious (and highly dangerous) Black Knight whose name is spoken of in terrified whispers throughout Avalon?

If you have previously travelled through the Wizard Ansalom's Dark Castle, go to **96**.
If you want to speak politely to the armoured figure, you may do so, then retreat prudently to your map and explore another part of the village.
If you want to make a name for yourself by challenging the Black Knight to a battle, go to **118**.

'That's a dangerous place to be going to be sure,' remarks the little man. 'And difficult to get to, if you don't know the way; although, then again, anywhere's difficult to get to if you don't know the way.'

'Do *you* know the way?' you ask quickly, this being the first indication that you may still be on the right road.

'I do that,' says the little man. 'At least in theory, for I've never been there meself and never want to either. But if you're determined, sure wouldn't I be a poor man if I didn't put you on the right track in token of your generosity. But I'm afraid you're going to have to go through that village yonder.'

'Why do you say "afraid"?' you ask, frowning.

'Because it's a place you'd do well to keep out of. Now, unlike the Dragon Cavern, I *have* been to Stonemarten Village – that being the name of the cursed place – and lucky I was to get away from it with a whole skin. Still, if you want to reach the Dragon Cavern, there's nothing else for it but to go through the Village.'

'I've been heading towards the village,' you tell him, 'but I don't seem to get any closer.'

'No, you wouldn't and that's for sure. There's only one way in, and a lot of folks miss it altogether. So it's lucky you are that you met me, for I can·tell you the right road.' With which he leans across and whispers something in your ear.

You thank the little man, pack up your belongings (taking care not to leave any litter) and trudge off in search of **13**.

57

Close up, this doesn't look nearly so impressive as it does at a distance. In fact, it doesn't look impressive at all. It looks decidedly seedy, if not exactly tumbledown. The sort of place that might have been a beautiful Abbey once, but has certainly seen better days. Past its prime, as you might remark. Over the hill. But still used, by the looks of this.

Approaching you, faces lost in the voluminous hoods of their voluminous robes are six — count them — black-clad Monks. The one in front carries an embroidered banner on a long pole. Your eyes move upwards to the banner. On it is a golden death's head. The one next to him carries a censor in which he appears to be burning old socks, to judge from the stench that is emerging from it. They turn towards you. They are chanting. What they are chanting is: 'Come with us, little adventurer, and stay with us forever.'

If you want to stay with them forever, go to **110**. If you run really fast now, you can go back to your map and explore some other part of the village. (The Monks will not follow outside their Abbey.) If you fancy your chances in a scrap, the good news is that the first two Monks will not take

57 Six black-clad Monks approach you

part whatever happens. The other four are Martial Monks each with 25 LIFE POINTS. They strike with bare hands for additional damage of +3. They move so fast all four will have a strike against you before you can do anything in return. And they hit on 4 or better. But it's your choice, Pip. If you fight and they kill you, go to **14**. If you fight and win, go to **94**.

58

You seem to be approaching a town, Pip. Well, a village, really. The first thing you see is the steeple of the village church, then later, as you continue trudging wearily along, the thatched roofs of the cottages come into sight.

The only thing is that however far you walk, you don't seem to be coming any nearer. You walk and walk without avail. The village is still there, but still distant. This has definitely the smell of magic, Pip. Better roll your magic dice to find out if there's some way in.

Score 2 – 4 and to to **9**.
Score 5 – 8 and go to **13**.
Score 9 – 12 and go to **19**.

59

A strong cross wind rises, making it exceptionally difficult for you to cling to the cliff face. Even using your equipment, this is a climb worthy of an expert mountaineer. Gusts pluck at your clothing, setting you swaying, threatening to send you crashing to your death. But you call up every ounce of strength and willpower you possess and hang on grimly. Your muscles knot with the effort and you hurt in every limb. But your steel determination and steely fingers win the day eventually . . .

Very well done indeed, Pip! You find yourself at the bottom of the chasm. Now there's only that little problem of the raging torrent at the bottom . . . You stare across the river, perhaps remembering for the first time that you don't know whether or not the body of Pip you occupy has ever learned to swim. And swimming is your only option here. Plunge bravely into the icy waters, Pip, then roll dice to find out what happens.

Score 2 – 6 and go to **68**.
Score 7 – 12 and go to **78**.

60

Haven't you anything better to do with yourself than waste time staring down a well, Pip? Especially a well with a Water Weird in it? That's right – a *Water Weird*!

This creature has only 10 LIFE POINTS, but if you think that's good news, think again – it can only be harmed by magic. You're going to have to use a P.A.D. or P.O.W. spell (if you have any left).

If either spell is successful, the creature dies and you can return to your map and continue exploring the village.

If the spell fails or you don't have any spells left, the creature will soak up your LIFE POINTS like a sponge. Go to **14**.

61

You know something? For the first time in this grotty village, you've actually found somewhere that *feels* nice. You stand just inside the doorway of the cottage, soaking up that very pleasant feeling.

If you have been running short on LIFE POINTS the cottage has restored you to *full strength*. How about that! What's more, you can return here after (but not during) any Section to get restored again, provided, of course, you are still in the village. Now go back to your map and explore somewhere else and don't complain nothing nice ever happens to you.

62

You proceed north for a short distance before discovering it was a bad old choice to make. The ground cracks abruptly beneath your feet, plunging you downwards into an underground lava stream. It's only a little stream, but that's neither here nor there. Even a little lava stream is quite enough to put paid to just about anybody.

Go to **14**.

63

As you approach this cottage you know at once it must be inhabited since there is a plume of smoke emerging from the chimney. Your suspicion is confirmed after you knock politely and a voice calls, 'Come in.'

There is something vaguely familar about that voice: not so much that you've heard it before, but rather that you've heard something like it before. You step inside and see, seated on a rocking chair beside the fire, clay pipe clamped firmly in his teeth, none other than . . . *an Old Residenter*!

'Thought you'd turn up here soon,' he remarks, eying you with a mixture of welcome, suspicion and resentment. 'Come looking for the Brass Dragon, have you?'

'Well, yes –' you begin to say. But like most Old Residenters, he talks more than he listens and already he is shaking his head.

'Well, you won't find it here, mark my words, young 'un. All the Omens are wrong.'

'No,' you begin to say, 'I didn't actually expect to find –'

'You want to have a look in Dragon Cavern,' he interrupts you. 'That's where it'll be most likely, if it isn't out ravaging and pillaging and eating Presbyterian Bishops and the like.'

'Well,' you say, 'actually, I was looking for Dragon Cavern. I don't suppose you happen to know where –'

'And don't ask me where Dragon Cavern might be,' interrupts the Old Residenter. 'I don't hold with places like that. They're immoral, so I avoids them.'

He stands up, clay pipe still clamped firmly in his teeth. 'You'll be wanting some stew, I'll be bound. Young 'uns your age are always hungry.'

'No really –' you begin politely, although the truth is you *are* a bit peckish.

'Thought so,' says the Old Residenter. 'I'll give you a bowl now and a bowl to take away, if you have anything to carry it in. It do have bay leaf and mugwort in it so that it will cure anything that ails you.'

'Healing stew?' you ask, eyeing the black pot on the fire.

'Aye, and don't sound so surprised. Don't you know the old saying:

> *When illness gnaws*
> *Or wounds and sores,*
> *The thing for you*
> *Is Residenter stew.'*

'Well, no,' you admit, 'I hadn't in fact heard that one.'

'Well you have now,' he tells you bluntly. 'A bowl of this will cure any illness, or any wound. You'll feel the LIFE POINTS rising like tree sap in spring.' And, using a ladle which was hanging on a nail beside the fire, he fills you a bowl.

Which bowl will naturally restore you to full LIFE POINTS if they happen to be depleted, and heal you of any illness you may have contracted in your adventure. What's more, if you had sense enough to bring cooking utensils, you can take a bowl of stew with you to eat later if you lose any more LIFE POINTS. (But you must have cooking utensils, since Old Residenter stew only works if eaten hot.) For now, return to the village map and continue your exploration.

64

It's lifted. The fog has lifted! How about that: your famous sense of direction wasn't too bad after all.

Now go direct to **58**.

65

You've trudged many miles north-east to get to
this place, Pip; and now you've got here, you may
be wondering why you bothered. Avalon's green
meadows and fertile fields gradually gave way to
wilder, rougher land until now you have reached
the edge of a dark, rather threatening wood. What
you notice most about it is the brooding stillness.
Birds usually twitter non-stop in woods, small
animals usually rustle through the undergrowth.
But nothing rustles here, and the only twittering
is the nervous beating of your heart. Are you going
to enter the wood, Pip?

If you decide NOT to enter the wood, and trudge back the way you came, turn to the Route Map to the Dragon Cavern and select a new direction *beginning from the start marked 'x'*.

If you decide to risk your neck by entering the wood, go to **5**.

66

Go direct to **41**.

67

'Welcome home,' says the monster, obviously having noticed you are gradually turning to stone. 'We've saved a very nice spot for you when you petrify completely. Over there to the south, where it's warm.'

You're not going to take that, are you, Pip? With a super-colossal effort of will you draw your sword and take a swipe. Somehow you're going to fight your way out, even if you die in the attempt.

The Stone Monster hasn't all that many LIFE POINTS since it's half dead already – just 18 to be exact. And it needs to score 7 or better to get a hit on you. What's more, your massive effort has given you the first strike. As against that, you're more or less half dead too, so you're fighting at a real disadvantage. You will need to score 8 or better to hit during this combat, and the fact that the monster is stone will deduct 1 from every damage score you make. Ah well, you might be lucky.

If the monster kills you, go to **14**.
If you manage to kill the monster, you may stagger back out of the stone garden, at which time your creeping paralysis will leave you. Go back to your map and explore a safer part of the village.

68

Blub . . . glug . . . glug . . . glug . . .

That's the sound of you drowning, Pip – the stupid body couldn't swim!

Go to **14**.

69

Go direct to **41**.

70

You're in luck, Pip. You totter backwards until your foot reaches the edge of the stone garden. At once the monster freezes, while you, by contrast, find that you have ceased to turn to stone. That was a close call!

Go back to your map and explore a safer part of the village.

71

Congratulations! You've found a horseshoe! Now stop wasting time.

Go back to your map and explore a more interesting part of the village.

72

It's made of stone! Solid stone! This cottage isn't a
cottage at all – it's a vast block of solid stone cut
to look like a cottage and thatched! Freaky!

Go back to your map and explore another part
of the village.

73

Now that's a bit better, Pip. Not much, but a bit.
The trees seem to be thinning out a little and . . .

Oh dear, you've met a Troll. Ugly little devil he is
too. The woods are full of them at this time of
year, so it really isn't too surprising – just
unfortunate, Trolls being what they are. Wood
Trolls anyway. They're quite immune to metal, so
it's no good trying to attack him with your

sword or other weapons. ('No good at all,' mumbles EJ.)

But if you don't attack him, he'll steal you blind. He'll have everything you carry (barring armour and weapons) if you don't do something quickly.

You've really only got three options. You can drown him in your waterbag. (You did bring a waterbag, didn't you?) The water will taste funny afterwards, but that's only to be expected. Or if you didn't bring a waterbag, you can hit him on the head with your spare boots. (You did bring spare boots, didn't you?) Or if you didn't bring a waterbag and spare boots, you can charm him by playing on your lute or harp. (You did bring a lute or harp, didn't you?)

> If you haven't the equipment to deal with the Wood Troll, you will lose everything you brought except for weapons and armour. Either way, go on to **11**.

74

Go direct to **41**.

75

'Welcome home,' says the Stone Monster.

But you make no reply. This is not stoicism in the face of danger. You make no reply because you can't! You've turned completely to stone!

Go to **14**.

76

You are a third of the way there . . .

You are halfway there . . .

Your muscles are now straining and aching from all your previous endeavours. Your legs feel like lead. Your fingers, numb from the river, refuse to function. You are losing your grip, Pip. You are *losing your grip*!

You are falling . . . falling . . . falling . . .

You fall all the way to **14**.

77

Good judgement, Pip.

Go to **21**.

78

You're in luck, Pip. This body can swim like a fish, like an otter! The icy torrent buffets you, sucks you under, throws you against hidden rocks . . . and still you swim on! The current hurls you back, pulls you forward . . . and still you swim on. Your skill and grim determination – not to mention your adventure-hardened muscles – win the day. You cross safely.

Now there's only that little problem of the sheer cliff face on the other side . . . Out with your climbing gear and roll two dice, Pip. Let's see if you make the final hurdle.

78 The icy torrent buffets you

Score 2 – 9 and go to **85**.
Score 10 – 12 and go to **76**.

79

Go direct to **41**.

80

A little perseverance goes a long way. You've spotted a doorway. Not a door, just a doorway – the door itself is long gone. But the doorway leads into the ruined tower. You draw your sword and edge carefully towards it, senses straining for any hint of danger. There is no sound; nothing at all. You enter.

It is gloomy in these ruins so that it takes a moment for your eyes to adjust. But eventually you see that the interior of the tower is in even worse condition than the outside. Fallen stones and heaps of rubble lie everywhere. There are the remains of a stone staircase spiralling upwards, but it doesn't go very far. You can see where the top fell in less than five metres above your head. For a moment you consider returning outside, but since you have come this far you decide to explore a little. Your sword still at the ready, you begin to move carefully through the rubble . . .

Once again your perseverance is rewarded! You see, half hidden by the rubble, a rotted wooden trap door, bound in rusty iron. There is an iron ring to lift it. You grip the ring firmly and heave. The ring comes away in your hand, but it doesn't matter: the whole door is so rotted, the metal so rusted that it all crumbles, leaving you staring down into a deep, dark shaft. Too dark to see.

Quickly you light a torch. The flickering light shows you steep stone steps leading downwards. Once again you hesitate, wondering if you should return to the sunshine outside. But what is there in the village for you? Are you not Pip, the Dragonslayer? Well, Pip the Prospective Dragonslayer anyway.

Bravely you step on to the stairway.

Bravely you slip and fall.

Bravely you dust yourself down when you reach the bottom, with no damage done fortunately. You are in an underground corridor, dark, dank, unlit. Will you follow it? Of course you will! Well, won't you?

If you don't wish to follow the corridor, return to your map and explore some other part of the village.
If, in fact, you do follow the corridor, turn to **25**.

81

This is a magical refuge, Pip. Lovely place it is too, although quite beyond description except to say there is a very great deal of blue light about. Bathe in the light, then return to the Section you have just left with your LIFE POINTS fully restored.

82

What's that noise? Somebody's whistling, just behind that tree. Maybe they know the way out of this stupid wood. Swiftly, you plunge through the undergrowth towards the sound. You reach the tree and dart behind it. Good grief! It's a Wolf! The whistling you heard was a wolf whistle!

Try for a Friendly Reaction. Quickly! If you don't get one, it's out with EJ –

('Fighting so soon?' EJ grumbles. 'Can't you give me any peace?')

– and into battle.

The whistling Wolf has 15 LIFE POINTS, but blunt teeth so he won't do you any more damage than shown on the dice roll.

If you win this battle or get a Friendly Reaction, go to **11**. If not, you're for the dreaded (or is it deaded?) **14**.

83

Go direct to **41**.

84

The smell of burning sulphur hangs heavily in the air, now joined by a second stench – the unmistakable odour of methane. You seem to be getting warm here, Pip: and that has nothing to do with the heat.

The path you are on ends in the yawning mouth of a great cavern. Not to put too fine a point on it,

84 The path to Dragon Cavern

you definitely seem to have found . . .

DRAGON CAVERN!!!

Don't suppose you want to go home now?

Thought not. Gird your loins and go to **95**.

85

You made it! After all that, you made it! You are safely across the chasm!

Go to **16**.

86

'No! No!' EJ shrieks in panic as you step forward. 'I have this dreadful premonition. I have a fearsome intuition. I have . . .'

But his voice trails away in astonishment.

The secret passage has led you into a vast, natural underground cavern, large as a cathedral and cut (to judge from the walls) by human hands right out of the bedrock underneath Stonemarten Village.

The cavern is entirely lit by luminous, glowing crystals embedded in the walls and in the natural stone pillars which support the roof. And beneath this roof, growing out of the stone floor, are crystal flowers and shrubs, mushrooms of every size, shape and colour, all translucent or transparent, all catching the light and glinting so that the whole place looks like Fairyland. Which it might well be, to judge by the little winged creatures which flit around the flowers. You stop, breathless at the sight.

The little winged creatures (could they *really* be fairies?) ignore you completely. But there is something else in this cavern, something larger and altogether more majestic. It is a tall, slender manlike figure with silver skin and huge golden eyes. Those eyes turn towards you the moment you enter. At your side, you feel EJ begin to quiver.

The creature – perhaps the most beautiful thing you have ever seen – walks towards you, stopping no more than ten metres distant. The golden eyes seem to stare directly into your very soul.

It speaks. 'Mortals who enter here are often obliged to stay forever.'

'I told you!' hisses EJ. 'You've really done it now!'

But the creature continues speaking, its melodious voice echoing within your mind. 'But I perceive your heart is pure and that your task is urgent. Therefore, you may take that which you seek and leave in peace.' And it turns away.

That which you seek? But you don't know what you want, do you Pip?

'Excuse me –' you call. 'Excuse me, sir?'

The regal creature turns again and waits.

'I'm afraid I don't quite know where I am,' you confess.

'You have reached the entrance to the Kingdom of the Sidhe. I see it is your fate that you may one day adventure here. But for the moment you may pass no further than this cavern.'

Which doesn't make a lot of sense. But you say hurriedly, 'I don't really want anything, you know. I sort of found this passage and was curious.' Then, on an inspiration you add, 'My sword told me to come here.'

The creature smiles. 'Perhaps so. And since you want nothing, it is the custom of my race to give you something. Please hand me your sword.'

'No!' screams EJ, then mercifully faints and falls silent.

Compelled by some unknown force, you hand EJ to the silver figure who strokes the blade briefly once, then hands it back to you. 'When your sword awakens he will be slightly changed. From this moment on, he will score +10 when fighting dragons. Go now.'

And this time, as he turns, the light begins to fade from the crystals. Hurriedly, you make your way back through the secret passage.

Quite something, that, Pip. Take a deep breath to calm yourself and return to your village map. And don't forget EJ now scores +10 damage against dragons.

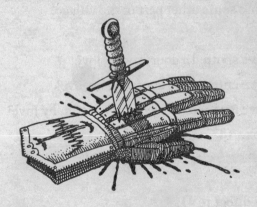

87

That is certainly one dead Phantom! By the time this adventure is over, everybody will be calling you Pip the Phantomslayer. If they aren't calling you Pip the Dragonslayer, of course. They might even be shaking their heads and saying, 'Poor old Pip. Did rather well, but the monsters got the best of it eventually.'

But enough of this. There's a church to search. And search it you do, but there's not a penny or a sovereign or a sixpence to be found anywhere, not even in the collection box. There is, however, a ring on the finger of the Phantom, which you carefully remove and put on your finger. It tingles as you do so. A tinglering? A magic ring?

You have no way of telling. Just be glad you got it and hope it may come in useful later. (It had better: you can't get it off your finger now.)

Press on, Pip! Press on! Return to your map and explore some other part of the village.

88

You've spotted a doorway, by Jove!

You've entered the doorway, by Jove!

You've just been buried by a cave-in, by Jove!

Go to **14**.

89

Go direct to **41**.

90

Thought you would.

The passage twists and turns quite a bit. It's very narrow and low ceilinged, so you spend most of your time bent nearly double with your elbows scraping the walls before you finally come to a dead stop against a blank wall. Surely it can't just end here?

No, of course it can't. You feel around until you find another funny little knob and when you turn that, the whole wall slides back with a grinding of stone on stone. (Isn't this exciting?) You are just about to step through when EJ whispers, 'Don't go in there!'

You hesitate. 'Why not?' you whisper back.

'I've been on more adventures than you,' EJ says pompously. 'There's always something nasty when you come out from secret passages. Always. It's a sort of Law of Nature, like gravity or the way you always have bits over if you take a clock to pieces and put it back together again. Don't go in there or it's Section **14** for sure.'

'But what am I supposed to do then?' you ask.

'Go back to your map and explore some other part of the village. Some safer part,' EJ urges.

So what are you going to do? Back to the village map? If you decide to ignore EJ, step out of the passage into **86**.

What ghastly corpse will emerge from the open grave? What mouldering monster? What vicious vampire? What ghostly ghoul?

'Avast there, Matie – give us a hand, then!'

It's either a very fresh corpse or the Gravedigger. You decide it must be the Gravedigger, and since he's the only relatively normal soul you've seen in

Stonemarten Village (apart from the fact he's crawling out of a grave, that is) you decide to give him a hand. And up he comes, a portly, bearded man with a distinctly florid face and nautical air about him, not to mention the scent of rum on his breath, which might explain how he came to fall into the open grave.

'Thank 'e kindly, me brave young gallant. A man in my condition doesn't find it all that easy to climb out of a grave. Cedric's the name. Long John Cedric they call me, on account of my seafaring background. At your service. Former Captain. Former pirate. Presently in retirement as a gravedigger.'

'I'm Pip,' you say, wondering if he's mad.

'Heered tell once of a Pip that put paid to the Wizard Ansalom. Hardly likely to be you, would it – ?' And before you have a chance to answer, he goes on: 'No, I thought not. Never mind, if you've stumbled into Stonemarten Village you'll be wondering what's the matter with the place. I'll tell you, since you were decent enough to help me out of the grave. It's cursed, that's what. The whole place, except for me. Couple of cottages turned to solid stone. The local banker was turned into a gnome. The Vicar is a Phantom now. All the horses ran away. Most of the ordinary folks got turned into stone monsters – petrified, you might say. And a very strange class of person started to move in. I'd have been in trouble meself if the rum hadn't protected me. Very hard to curse a man with rum in him. At least that's my theory.' His eyes are glazed, as if the mention of rum had sent the liquor recirculating through his system.

'Who cursed the village?' you ask excitedly.

But he is already collapsing with the drink. As he sinks to the ground and slowly rolls back into the open grave, you catch one muttered word: 'Dragons. . .'

'Dragons?' you shout. 'What about dragons?'

But your only reply is a snore from the open grave. Better return to your map and explore some more of the village: you won't get anything else here.

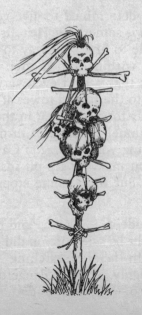

92

You step through the doorway into fog. At once you turn, but even your lightning reflexes are not fast enough. There is no sign of the door. You fumble in the fog without avail. You fumble for a very, very long time.

Go to **8**.

93

This may well be a Gnome of Zurich, Pip – you wouldn't believe the way he counted and recounted your money before stashing it carefully away in a leather pouch with a lock on it. Imagine! A locked pouch!

But he seems determined to give good value for money, which is something. He tells you that it is indeed possible to find your way to the Dragon's Cavern from within Stonemarten Village; and also mentions that it isn't even very far. All you need do is go to the ruined tower at **30** and there search carefully for a trap door in the floor which leads into a tunnel, leading, in turn, to the path which will bring you to Dragon Cavern. Excited as you are, you make to zip off instantly to the ruined tower. But the Gnome stops you with a gesture.

'One word of advice,' he says, 'and free of charge at that. It might be safest if you did not go to the Dragon Cavern before searching Stonemarten Village thoroughly. This is a dangerous place, as I know only too well, but it does have hidden

somewhere one or two items which may mean
the difference between life and death when you
enter the Cavern. *Your* life and death, that is.'

But what are these items and where shall I find
them?' you cry.

The Gnome shakes his gnomish head. 'King
Arthur himself would not have enough gold in the
Royal Treasury to pay for that information.' And
he nods politely and disappears into his cottage,
closing the door behind him.

When you try to follow (as you most certainly do),
you find the door, which looks like wood, is in
fact some hardened form of metal, while the
windows are of some magically toughened glass
which is quite unbreakable. The cottage is as
secure as a bank vault. Nothing else for it, since
the Gnome refuses to come out, but to return to
your map of Stonemarten Village, and make your
decision on whether to explore further or to go
directly to the ruined tower. . .

94

Before King Arthur chased the Romans out, there
was a saying current throughout Avalon (which
was not called Avalon then, of course), and this
saying went: 'To the Victor, the Spoils'. (*Ad victor
spoilarum* or some such nonsense in the original
Latin.) It is a saying which applies fully to you
now, Pip, for you were undoubtedly victorious in
hacking up those morbid monks. So don't waste

another moment: get into the Abbey and search, search, search. Roll two dice to discover what, if anything, you find.

Score 2–4 and go to **115**.

Score 5–8 and go to **119**.

Score 9–12 and go to **106**.

Behind you, the volcanic wasteland. Before you, the mouth of a dark, gloomy, yawning cavern. In your nostrils, the scent of dragon and the smell of sulphur fumes and methane gas. In your hand (if you have any sense at all) your trusty sword. In your mind a knowledge of your spells.

This is it, Pip. This is the place you have searched for for so long, the place you risked your life to find. If there were trumpeters here, they would blow a huge triumphant fanfare to the heavens; although it's perhaps as well that there are not, for the last thing you need is a stampede of dragons, Brass or otherwise, disturbed by a blast of trumpet music.

You edge forward, senses alert, heart pounding. Questions cascade unbidden into your mind. Will the Brass Dragon really be hiding here? Merlin seems to think so, but he could be wrong. How many other dragons will you find here? Everyone in Avalon knows this cavern is the home of a large number of the monsters. What else is in the warren of underground tunnels, corridors, caves and caverns you are about to enter? Legend speaks of creatures so ghastly that they can live unmolested by the firebreathers, creatures so terrifying that even dragons leave them alone.

It is enough to daunt all but the most valiant heart. Which is why it is to your eternal credit, Pip, that you take a firm step forward and

Go to **108**.

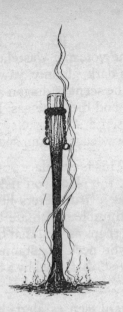

No, of course it's not! It's somebody you remember from your adventure in the Wizard Ansalom's Dark Castle. The last time you saw him was at King Arthur's Court in Camelot, dressed in all his finery and insignia of rank. And the time before that he was lost in the woods outside the Dark Castle, bravely determined to do something about the Wizard if he ever found his way out again. A man worthy of respect, Pip, as all true kings are, but one whose bark is definitely worse than his bite.

'King Pellinore?' you ask. 'Is it you, Your Majesty?'

'What?' asks the black-armoured figure. 'What?

What? What? By Jove, I know you, don't I? Young Pip, the fearless adventurer, no less. Am I right? What?'

'Well, I don't know about fearless. . .' you say modestly.

'Nonsense! They're still talking about your last exploit all over the country. Even the Scots have heard about it and you know how long it takes them to catch on to anything. Shouldn't be surprised if it gets through to Hibernia in a year or two. Well, Pip, what brings you to this godforsaken place?'

'I'm in search of Dragon Cavern,' you tell him. 'I was following a map Merlin drew and it led me here.'

'Wouldn't put too much faith in Merlin's maps,' Pellinore remarks. 'I was following one of his myself when I got lost looking for the Wizard Ansalom.'

'I don't suppose you would know where the Dragon Cavern is, by any chance?' you ask.

''Fraid not, young friend. To tell you the truth, I've been having so much difficulty finding a way out of this place that I commandeered a cottage to live in until I worked out the right route. But I did come across one thing that might help you.' And from the sleeve of his armour he withdraws a rolled scroll. 'It's a description of the Cavern itself, about the sort of place it is. Might come in useful to know what you're facing if you do find your way there.' With which he hands you the scroll.

To read what it says go to **101**, then to your map of Stonemarten Village in order to continue your exploration.

97

Feeling better now, Pip? You certainly should be. It seems your sturdy young body is not only handsome, well-proportioned, fine-muscled and good to look upon, but also immune to this particular type of poison. All the same, you should be careful about tucking away so many jam tarts, otherwise you'll get fat.

Now return to your map and continue exploring Stonemarten Village. More cautiously this time.

98

The corridor – a natural fissure in the rock by all appearances – twists, turns, widens, then narrows until you have almost lost all sense of direction. (Although your experience suggests it generally runs roughly north-west.) Eventually the passage narrows to such a degree that you are actually forced to turn sideways in order to pass through it.

You are squeezing through the last few metres when you emerge, like a cork from a bottle, into another cavern, larger than the entrance cavern. Marching through this cavern is a contingent of tiny, ugly, large-headed humanoid creatures, each armed with a sword and wearing leather armour. There is no doubt in your mind that you have met up with a party of Rock Trolls. There is a second passage leading out of this cavern to the north, rather wider than the one by which you entered. But how to reach it?

Your Invisibility spell can work here. If you get your roll and use it successfully, you may creep quietly past the Trolls and leave by the northern passage to **99**. But remember this spell can be used only once and you may need it later.

You might try introducing yourself and hoping to convince the Trolls to let you past. If so, go to **103**.

You may fancy your chances of hacking them to bits. There are six Trolls in all. Each has 10 LIFE POINTS. They haven't seen you, so you can get in first strike against one of them. The others will, however, strike back in sequence before you can strike again. They hit on 6, with +2 damage on their swords. Their armour, which isn't very good, will absorb only 1 point of damage you score against them. Get your dice rolling if you pick this option. If you kill the Trolls, you may proceed to **99**. If they kill you, it's **14**.

99

The passageway, which looks as though it has been used fairly often, runs in a two hundred metre stretch to a vast cavern notable mainly for the almost overpowering stench which emerges from it. Your torch soon shows the cause of the smell: the centre of the cavern floor is piled high with dragon droppings. Your hand drops instantly to your sword hilt, but a moment's quick inspection convinces you there are no dragons about at the moment. As you stand in the centre of the cave (just short of the manure heap) there are three exits.

West will take you to **98**.

North will take you to **105**.

East is almost totally blocked by a large boulder. If you wish to try this direction, roll two dice to find out if you are strong enough to move the boulder. Score 2–6 and it won't shift, so you must choose another way. Score 7–12 and though it's heavy, you manage to shift it sufficiently to squeeze past, in which case go to **102**. Note: if you wish to use one of your precious Fireballs here, it will, on a hit, crumble the boulder to dust, allowing you to go to **102**.

If you decide to search the heap of dragon dung (what a revolting thought) before leaving this cavern, go to **111**.

100

You've got a bit of a tummy ache, Pip. And it's getting worse. Maybe you shouldn't have scoffed so many of those jam tarts. Or those cakes. Or maybe. . .maybe the food is poisoned!

99 A large boulder blocks your way

Yeech! It *is* poisoned! You can feel the poison creeping through you, invading every cell and fibre of your body. This is no fun. Grab your dice and find out if it is going to send you back to the dreaded **14**.

Score 2–6 and go to **97**.

Score 7–12 and go to **109**.

101

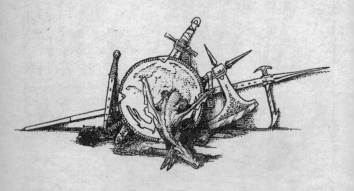

Be it known to all adventurers that I, Ethelbert, warrior monk and loyal subject of Arturus Rex, son of Uthur Pendragon and rightful Liege Lord of the Realm of Avalon, do hereby testify in verity and truth that I, the said Ethelbert, have by the grace of God and a strong right arm, reached that place which men call Dragon Cavern and ventured a distance therein. Soon I must venture within this dreadful place again, risking my sanity and my very life, and so I write this scroll lest I perish, that it might be an aid to any who may come after me to this accursed place.

First, the approach is across a volcanic wasteland, cliff-enclosed, so that only two routes are open to the traveller. One leads to the Cavern, the other is certain death. Avoid the more obvious road and you will reach the Cavern.

The Cavern itself is unmistakable by reason of its size and smell, which is the foul smell of brimstone and dragon breath. You may venture in reasonable safety within the first cavern, for the dragons nest far below in the accursed labyrinth and there is little here save the picked bones of those who have perished. From the first cavern you will discover there is a choice of routes. None is safe, for all lead into the maze of corridors and tunnels which have been cut over the aeons through living rock into the very bowels of the earth.

It has been said that strange creatures other than the dragons roost in the labyrinth, and this I have discovered to be true. It may be that some of these races are friendly: I cannot say, for I have met none that were not dangerous indeed. There are things here which men speak of in whispers, things which the wise and learned believe to be a myth. But they are not myths: this I affirm and attest, for I have seen them with my own eyes, fought them with my sword and monkish spells. To my certain knowledge, there is a race of trolls, a clan of hunchbacked dwarves, a foul creature like unto a man but having the head of a bull, a snake woman, and a wailing spirit which can take the life of an adventurer with a single touch. I pray you meet none of these monsters, for I have met them and it was only God's grace which allowed me to escape with my life. There may be others. I do not know, although I suspect there are. Perhaps I shall discover them when I venture in again.

These creatures share the dragon's lair, avoiding the great firebreathers when they can. The dragons themselves roost in the lower levels, although there is always the danger that one or more may take to the corridors in order to leave the Cavern. It is a small danger, admittedly, for when they wish to feed or mate, they will normally fly upwards, emerging out of a great natural chimney on the clifftop.

But if you avoid the dragons in the corridors, you will not avoid them in the lower levels. They teem there like ants, far more of them than was ever suspected in Avalon. Tread softly and warily, brave adventurer. I may not live to tell my own tale, but I pray you live to tell yours. If you succeed, remember me at matins and at vespers, in token of the aid I have given you in this writing. I append my name.

Ethelbert. Monk and Warrior.

102

The corridor takes you without mishap to a small, apparently empty cave. The exits are:

South to **108**.

North-west to **99**.

East to **112**.

A flicker at the corner of your eye! You spin round, but there is nothing there. Another flicker. You turn again. Still nothing there. Something touches your left arm, chilling it to the bone. For the briefest instant you are staring into the glowing, ethereal eyes of a Wraith. Then the creature vanishes instantly.

A Wraith? Those things are deadly. And they can only be fought with spells: physical weapons do them no damage whatsoever. The Wraith is attacking you, Pip. That single touch cost you 10 LIFE POINTS! (If this kills you, go to **14**.) You must use your spells! The Wraith has 25 LIFE POINTS. It will strike back successfully on a roll of 6 or better, scoring +3 damage at a touch.

If you kill the Wraith you may choose your exit.

If the Wraith kills you, go to **14**.

103

Roll two dice.

Score 2–9 and the Trolls, an aggressive bunch, are beyond all reasoning. Return to **98** and reconsider your options.

Score 10–12 and the Trolls will let you past. Go
to **99**.

104

There is a rustling in the grain. A *loud* rustling.
Yuk! It's Rats! There must be hundreds of them to
judge by the noise. No there aren't There's one!
And it's the size of an Irish wolfhound! It stares at
you momentarily with pink, glittering eyes and
gnashes teeth like daggers. Look out, Pip, it's
launching itself upon you! Roll dice quickly to
find out if you can get in a quick sword thrust!

The Irish Wolfrat has a full 25 LIFE POINTS and bites at +2 on a score of 5 or better.

If the Rat kills you, go to **14**.

If you kill the Rat, go back to your map of Stonemarten Village and explore somewhere else. But NOTE: the Rat's bite carries disease, so that if it has even one successful strike against you, you must obtain healing before you leave the village otherwise you die. Look carefully in all the cottages. There must be some healing potions stashed away somewhere. Mustn't there?

105

You find yourself near the entrance of another cavern. There is, however, a branch passage on your right.

To enter the cavern go to **114**.

To take the corridor to your right, go to **120**.

106

What a find! What a find! It's a map of Dragon Cavern! At least, it's part of a map. When (and if) you reach the Cavern, you may refer to this map to help you find your way. It does not show the entrance, but it does show a section of the labyrinth, so it could save your life.

The map is shown opposite. You may refer to it at any time after you leave this Section. Now return to your map of Stonemarten Village and continue your explorations.

107

The interior of the crypt is hung with black velvet drapes in remarkably good condition, while the floor, walls and ceiling are all in the very finest white marble. In the centre of the floor is a small dais and on it an ebony coffin with gleaming brass inlay. There is an inscription on the dais which reads:

> *Wearily you journeyed on*
> *All hope near gone*
> *But now you're here*
> *On your last breath*
> *In the hope of finding someone dear*
> *Or death*

You groan inwardly at the standard of the verse (although all the while recalling that if this really *is* the Poetic Fiend, then you must be very careful to praise his poetry when he awakes) and climb up on the dais. Sure enough, there is a brass plaque set into the lid of the coffin, bearing the following inscription:

To awaken the Fiend, speak aloud the answer to this riddle:

WHAT'S THE DIFFERENCE BETWEEN A DUCK?

Speak your answer aloud now.

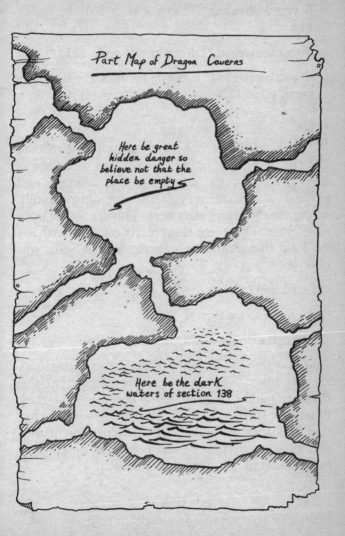

If you answered, 'That's a stupid riddle' go to **116**.

If you answered, 'I don't know' go to **121**.

If you answered, 'One of its legs are both the same' go to **122**.

108

You are within a bone-dry natural cavern, the floor of which is liberally scattered with bones and skulls, many animal, some human, and several of creatures you do not immediately recognise. Nothing stirs here. You are aware only of silence. There are three exits on the northern wall of this entrance cavern. Which will you choose?

Left-hand exit: go to **98**.

Right-hand exit: go to **99**.

Centre exit: go to **102**.

And just one more thing, Pip. The exit corridors are narrow. As you examine them in the flickering light of your torch you see that they twist and turn. In your heart of hearts you know that this may be your fateful choice. For in this part of your adventure, there will be no turning back. Onward. To glory. . .or to death!

109

Writhe in agony, Pip – you're definitely poisoned.

Go to **14**.

110

Sucker. You just got yourself sacrificed by the Monks. Want all the gory details? Perhaps not. Just go to **14**.

111

You've found a ring! It fits neatly on the finger of your left hand. The trouble is, now you've tried it, you can't get it off. And it tingles slightly.

A tinglering. Wonder what a tinglering actually *does*? But never mind that now. Go to **99** and decide where to go from there.

112

The passageway opens abruptly so that you find yourself standing on the rocky shore of a vast underground lake. There is no road around these still, dark waters. But there is, at least, a rather battered, leaky rowboat tied up only a few metres away from you.

If you have previously discovered on this adventure that you can swim, you might like to try swimming the lake. (If you don't know whether you can swim, don't risk it.) To attempt to swim, go to **123**.

If you want to risk that rowboat (although it does look very leaky) go to **117**.

113

After counting your money very carefully indeed, the Gnome tells you that there are two ways out of the village. Two of the cottages have back doors and either back door will get you beyond the stockade.

'But which cottages?' you ask.

'That will cost you a further 500 Gold Pieces,' says the Gnome, snidely.

'No it won't!' you exclaim, half drawing your sword with a threatening gesture.

'No, of course it won't,' agrees the Gnome. 'Only joking. Can't you take a joke?'

'The cottages?' you ask again, grimly.

'Yes, yes – the cottages. **38** and **43**. Either one.' With which he scurries back into his home and locks the door behind him.

> Return to your map of Stonemarten Village and go where you will. (Or possibly where thou wilt, as they say in this day and age.)

What a maggoty little cavern! Low roof, no exit and the whole place is positively full of some sort of nasty fungus. Smelly, nasty. . . Fungus.

Even at this very minute it's eating its way through your leg!

Run Pip! Too late – your leg has fallen off! The fungus is eating your head.

Go to **14**.

114 Fungus is eating your leg

What a find! What a find! You have discovered a scroll. And this is what it says:

Be it known that I, Ethelbert, monk, warrior and loyal subject of Arturus Rex, son of Uthur Pendragon and rightful Liege Lord of the Realm of Avalon, have, by the grace of God and a strong right arm, come thus far in my quest for the place men call Dragon Cavern.

And be it known that I, having found myself trapped for several months in the accursed Stonemarten Village with its foul magics and other perils, have at last discovered a true route herefrom, leading, so I believe, directly to the entrance of Dragon Cavern.

Thus I take up my quill and write this knowledge lest I perish on my quest, so that it may be of some small usage to any brave adventurer who follows me. The route, written plainly, is thus:

First go to the ruined tower and there search diligently for an entrance. When the entrance is found, enter and again search diligently. Within the rubble, half buried, is a rotted wooden trap door. This open and stone steps will be revealed. Be not afeared, but descend and follow the route. Soon you will emerge to daylight and a foul, cliff-enclosed place, a wasteland of hardened lava. This, as I attest, is the road to Dragon Cavern. Remember me at matins for this small service. I append my name.

Ethelbert, monk and warrior.

Now return to your map of Stonemarten Village
and explore further or follow the directions on
the scroll.

116

At once the coffin lid slams back and a slim,
deathly pale figure dressed in an evening suit and
opera cloak leaps out with alarming speed. His
eyes are pink and his top teeth jut out over his
lower lip. What's more, he looks cross.

'Stupid, is it?' cries the Fiend. 'I suppose you'll be
telling me my poetry is stupid too?'

'No, no!' you protest, remembering the Fiend's
fearsome reputation if anyone fails to praise his
execrable poetry. 'I am your most fervent and
devoted admirer as a poet. I feel you are one of the
all-time great poets of the known universe, totally
outclassing such lesser souls as Shakespeare,
Milton, Keats, Yeats, Shelley and even William
MacGonigle!'

The Fiend looks somewhat mollified at this,
although there remains a dangerous glint in his
eye. 'Very well,' he says, 'I shall forgive you, but
only on one condition. . .'

'On any condition, Poetic Fiend!' you cry bravely,
prepared to undertake any peril to get on the right
side of this peculiar (but definitely magical)
creature.

'You must draw my portrait,' says the Fiend

smugly. 'Use this. . .' And he hands you a blank sheet of parchment.

Better get working on the portrait, Pip. Use your imagination to create a Fiend worthy of hanging in the London Museum. Or a cemetery.

117

You climb into the rowboat and fish out the oars from the scummy pool of water in the bottom, fit them into the rowlocks and pull away from shore. The dark water swallows up the light from your torch, which you have jammed at the prow, so that you seem to be rowing through an endless night. Water from the boat's many leaks is already lapping around your feet as you strive to cross the lake before this old tub sinks. Roll two dice to find out if you make it safely.

Score 2–4 and go to **124**.

Score 5–12 and go to **132**.

118

Quickly you scrabble through your belongings looking for a gauntlet, and finding none seize the metal gauntlet which is lying on the cottage table. Quickly you fling the gauntlet in the visored face of the Black Knight in time-honoured challenge to single combat.

'Here, steady on!' exclaims the Black Knight. 'What do you think you're doing!'

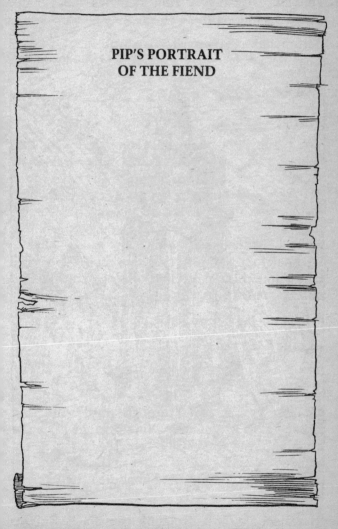

**PIP'S PORTRAIT
OF THE FIEND**

When finished go to **127**

118 The dreaded Black Knight of Avalon

'I'm challenging you to single combat!' you reply, your hand itching for its sword.

'Why would you want to do that?'

'Because,' you say, 'you are the dreaded Black Knight whom men speak of in whispers as the most verily evil Knight in the Realm, and I wish to rid Avalon of your putrid presence!'

'Don't be ridiculous,' says the Black Knight. 'I'm King Pellinore.' With which he removes his helmet and proves it.

What a *faux pas*! What a bloomer! King Pellinore is one of King Arthur's most trusted friends. If you hadn't been so hasty he might have been able to help you. As it is, you can only scrape and bow and cringe and fawn and apologise profusely as you back out of the cottage and return to your map of Stonemarten Village to explore some other Section.

119

Nothing. You find nothing at all. So much for stupid Roman sayings about victors and spoils. *Nihil ad Victor* as the more sensible Romans used to say: the Victor gets zilch.

Go back muttering to your map of Stonemarten Village and explore some more.

120

The passageway runs due east for a time then curves, first north-east, then, with increasing sharpness, north. You catch a strange odour, a little like that of the cattle shed at the home of your adoptive parents, but more pungent and somehow strangely menacing. Nonetheless you press on. Pip is not an adventurer for nothing. What is a little danger between friends? (S)he who hesitates is lost. Press on regardless. . .

While such daft thoughts are drifting through your mind, you reach the end of the passage and step directly into another cavern. There is an exit on the north wall, another to the east, and three large brass-bound chests and a small matching casket on the floor some five metres ahead of you. This would be an interesting and intriguing place to explore at your leisure were it not for one thing. Between you and the chests (not to mention the exit passage) is a two metres tall, heavily muscled figure, holding a naked sword. Except you aren't looking at the sword right now, however threatening it might be: you are looking at the figure's head which, incredibly, is that of a bull! You have entered the cave of the *MINOTAUR*!

'HALT!' bellows the Minotaur, making a curious scraping gesture with his right foot on the floor. 'NO ONE PASSES THIS WAY!'

'Keep your voice down, you silly monster!' you reply, perhaps with more bravado than you actually feel. 'I have no quarrel with you – I'm simply trying to find the Brass Dragon.'

'You?' snorts the Minotaur. 'A little pipsqueak like you looking for the Brass Dragon?'

'I am no pipsqueak,' you answer proudly, 'although my name is Pip. Perhaps you have heard of me?'

The Minotaur shakes his huge head, snorting. 'Can't say I have.'

'Then,' you say, 'you may have heard of the man who sent me – Merlin, the greatest magician in all Avalon.'

'Merlin, is it? I thought he'd be dead of old age by now.'

'Very much alive,' you say quickly, on the principle that jaw-jaw is safer than fight-fight, especially when you're facing anything as tough looking as a Minotaur.

'And you really know him? Personally?'

'Of course.'

The Minotaur stops scraping his foot on the ground. 'Do you think you could persuade him to fix my head?'

'What's wrong with your head?' you ask, wondering if the monster has a headache.

'It's shaped like the head of a bull,' says the Minotaur. 'Hadn't you noticed?'

'Well, yes. . .' you admit.

The Minotaur sits down on one of the chests and leans his sword against his knee. The great bull's head hangs sorrowfully. 'Most people do,' he remarks. He looks up. 'You don't think I was born like this, do you?' And before you can answer, he goes on: 'No, of course not. I was a perfectly normal child, good-looking as you are. I lived in Athens – a little Greek village you may have heard of. My head grew like this because I ate too many hamburgers, I think. I'm not altogether sure, but it's the only reason I can think of. All my friends deserted me, and while the King of Crete was decent enough to give me a job for a time guarding his labyrinth, the pay was appalling and eventually I turned it all in to come and skulk here. Do you think Merlin could cure me?'

'I'm sure he could,' you say. 'He's very good at changing the shape of things.'

'If you can get him to do it,' says the Minotaur, 'I'd be ever so grateful.'

'Would you let me pass through your cave unharmed?' you ask warily.

'I can't do that. Anyone who comes in here has to fight me – that's tradition. But we can make it a token fight with no weapons. First one to knock off 10 LIFE POINTS is the winner. If you win, you can go on through: I'll even let you search these chests for anything useful. If you lose, you have to go straight back to Merlin and see about fixing my head – how does that suit you?'

'That's suits me fine!' you say (in some relief). 'Shall we fight now?'

'Yes, let's!' says the Minotaur excitedly, leaping to his feet.

120 The Minotaur leaps to its feet

Roll two dice to decide the outcome of the fight. The Minotaur needs a six to hit, exactly as you do since this is a fist fight. First roll decides who gets first strike.

If you win, go to **126**.

If you lose, go to **133**.

121

At once the coffin lid slams back and a slim, deathly pale figure dressed in an evening suit and opera cloak leaps out with alarming speed. His eyes are pink and his top teeth jut out over his lower lip. What's more, he looks cross.

'You don't know?' screams the Fiend. 'What sort of answer is that? Everybody knows one of its legs are both the same!' With which he slams down the lid of his coffin and no attempts you make will persuade him to come out again.

Return to your map of Stonemarten Village and explore some other Section.

122

At once the coffin lid slams back and a slim, deathly pale figure dressed in an evening suit and opera cloak leaps out with alarming speed. His eyes are pink and his top teeth jut out over his lower lip – even when he is smiling, which he is now.

'Well done, my dear brave visitor! Well done! I could not have answered the riddle better myself.

Except in rhyme, of course. Something along the following lines:

> *'It was the riddle of the sphynx:*
> *What is the difference between a duck?*
> *That one is easy, I thinks*
> *And so I am in luck.*
> *And ever game*
> *I look the sphynx right in the eye*
> *And answer: One of its legs are both the same!'*

'There,' says the Fiend, eyes gleaming. 'What do you think of that as a poetic answer?'

'Magnificent!' you breathe, remembering the Fiend likes to be flattered about his poetry. 'I felt the mythological allusions were particularly apposite.'

'Yes,' says the Fiend, obviously pleased, 'so did I. Now, as you are clearly a young person of taste and discernment, let me give you an award for your intelligence.'

With which he takes from the pocket of his opera suit a small silver snuffbox. 'Do you take snuff?' he asks.

You shake your head.

'Good,' nods the Fiend. 'A filthy habit and most unhealthy. However, you may make an exception of *this* snuff. It's not made of tobacco, but rather of ground mugwort blessed by a vicar of the Anglican Communion. This gives it amazing healing properties. Take a pinch when you are feeling low and roll two dice twice. The total is the number of LIFE POINTS restored to you up to your natural maximum. But you may only use the snuff once in any Section, otherwise it will send you directly to **14**. Got that? Good. Now on your way, adventurer bold, for it is cold and I must get back into my coffin before I catch a chill and start coughin'.'

And he slams down the lid, leaving you with the snuffbox of healing stuff.

Go back to your map of Stonemarten Village and explore further. And don't lose that snuffbox! In fact, make a note that you have it.

123

You carefully remove your clothes and tie them up into a bundle, before plunging into the icy waters of the underground lake into the jaws of a very large Fish lurking in the depths!

This could be rather tricky, Pip. Old EJ is tied up in the bundle, so you're going to have to try to strangle that Fish with your bare hands. (Or knock it senseless, or whatever you do with fish.) It only has 10 LIFE POINTS, which doesn't sound too difficult, but the problem is you're *under water*, which means you have to get rid of the Fish within three combat rounds otherwise you'll drown. Meanwhile, the Fish will be biting you, which won't do your own LIFE POINTS much good.

If you manage to stun or kill the Fish in three rounds, go to **124**. If not, there's always **14**.

124

You have strong arms, Pip. Or maybe just a lot of luck. Whichever way, you made it! You squelch off across the cavern floor to the entrance of an exit passageway to the east.

Enter the passageway and go to **130**.

125

Go to **10**.

126

'Well now,' says the Minotaur (a little breathlessly after the fight), 'now that we've got that out of the way, you'd better have a rummage through my belongings. That's traditional too, you know. To the victor the spoils, as young Julius Caesar used to say to me before my head got this way and we stopped speaking to one another. But I'd better warn you, it's been set up so you can only look in two of them: once you do that, the others vanish. A little magic I bought to protect my belongings, you appreciate, except I don't know how to switch it off, so you're stuck with it, I'm afraid. Now we've got three chests and a casket. You can look in any two. So make your choice.'

You stare from chest to chest. They all three look

identical. The casket, although much smaller, is of essentially the same design. 'Can't you simply tell me what's in them?' you ask the Minotaur.

But he shakes his great bull's head. 'Tradition, you know . . .' he explains sadly. Since there's no way of telling the chests apart, Pip, let's call them 1, 2 and 3.

Open Chests 1 and 3 and go to **135**.
Open Chests 1 and 2 and go to **140**.
Open Chests 2 and 3 and go to **146**.
Open Chest 1 and the casket and go to **143**.
Open Chest 2 and the casket and go to **150**.
Open Chest 3 and the casket and go to **129**.

'What a fine work!' exclaims the Poetic Fiend. 'What a sterling effort! Almost equal, in certain respects, to the promise of my own early work. I am somewhat reminded of T.S. Eliot in his Blue Period (or was that Picasso?). Whoever. It is a magnificent effort and deserves some reward even though you got the riddle wrong.'

And he reaches into a pocket of his opera cloak to pull out a boiled sweetmeat on a stick. 'Have a lollipop!'

'A lollipop?' you ask, surprised. (And perhaps a little disappointed, if the truth be told.)

'A magic lollipop,' grins the Fiend, his fangs flashing slightly. 'Suck it and see. But not now, since you won't want to waste it. You only get three licks of the lollipop before it disappears forever. But each time you lick it – during a battle or some such confrontation – any LIFE POINTS you have lost are returned to you up to your natural maximum, while precisely the same number of LIFE POINTS are deducted from your opponent. A little difficult to calculate, but extremely useful if you are getting the worst of matters. And now ...' Here he begins to climb back into his coffin. ' ... I fear I must leave you, however pleasant this conversation has been.' With which, he pulls down the lid.

You knock on it tentatively, but there is no answer other than a muffled:

'Farewell, young Friend
Let's hope this is not the end
Of your great quest
For as my guest
Though others rave
You are certainly worthy of reaching Dragon
Cave!'

Go back to your map of Stonemarten Village
and explore some other Section.

128

You trip gaily along this passage without a care in
the world until you fall down a pit trap.

Roll two dice to determine the damage caused
by the fall. Subtract the result from your
current LIFE POINTS. If this kills you, go to **14**.
If you have a rope and spikes in your
equipment, you may use them to climb out
again. If not, you're stuck: starve for a week
then go to **14**.
If you get out of the pit, you may proceed. The
passage you're in leads to **120** in one direction
and **130** in the other.

129

How interesting. The casket contains a large key.
The chest, by contrast, is empty except for a
scroll. The scroll reads:

J FUIFMCFSU, NPOL BOE XBSSJPS, IBWJOH
CFGSJFOEFE UIF CFBTU XJUI UIF DPX'T IFBE
EP BUUFTU UIBU POMZ UIF LFZ XJUIJO UIF

DBTLFU XJMM QFSNJU BENJUUBODF UP UIF
MBJS PG UIF GJSFCSFBUIFST.

Which isn't very enlightening unless you can
manage to decode it.

As the Minotaur predicted, the remaining chests
have vanished. The passages from the Minotaur
cave lead to **114**, **128** and **137**.

Take your pick!

Wow!

This must be your lucky day, Pip. As you step into
a cave your torchlight illuminates the largest heap
of gems, silver, gold, electrum, jade, ivory and
artifacts you have ever seen. There is a king's
ransom here, a treasure beyond the wildest
dreams of avarice. This cavern makes the Wizard
Ansalom's fabled treasure house look like the
small-change booth in a second-rate circus. There
must be millions here: maybe billions. Diamonds,
rubies, sapphires, emeralds, circons, pearls . . .
hundreds of them, thousands of them just sitting
there in a huge pile waiting to be shovelled into a
backpack! This must be the legendary Dragon's
Treasure – ransom money for freed maidens,
treasure trove from ravaged monasteries and
castles, all the booty collected over centuries by
generations of rampaging dragons. All of it here,
all of it just waiting for a brave adventurer like
you. This could make such a difference to your

lifestyle, Pip. This could buy you a castle – a dozen castles. This could . . . but you know full well what this could do.

All you have to do to get it (as much as you can carry, at least, which is still an awful lot) is to persuade the lady with the funny-looking hair to let you take it. The lady with the funny-looking hair? That isn't hair on her head – it's snakes! Could this be the Medusa, the mythical female whose very look turns people to stone? Now you come to mention it, there are several very lifelike statues standing around near the heap of treasure. But think of all that loot, Pip. Think what you could do with it.

To grab some of this treasure, you're going to have to fight the Medusa. If you decide to do so, go to **136**.

If you feel discretion might be the better part of valour (and who needs loot anyway?) you may use your Invisibility spell to get out of this cave without being seen.

If you don't want to use your Invisibility spell here, you can try *creeping* out ever so quietly. To find out if you have succeeded, roll two dice. Score 2 – 6 and you're out without being spotted. Score 7 – 12 and the Medusa glanced briefly in your direction: go to **14**.

The passages out of this cavern lead to **138** and **128**.

130 Medusa is going to turn you into stone

131

Each nasty Dwarf has 10 LIFE POINTS. They are slow movers, so you can certainly have the first strike against some of them. Roll two dice to find out how many you can hit first. (If you manage a 12, it means you can take one bash at every one of them before *any* of them gets to strike you back.) When you have taken your first hit or hits, the Dwarves will strike you back in sequence. They aren't particularly good fighters and need 8 or better to hit. As against that, they are armed with swords which do +3 damage.

> If the Dwarves kill you, go to **14**.
> If you manage to kill ten of the Dwarves, the other two will run off in the direction of the Minotaur's cave, leaving you to do what you will in this cavern. Go to **134**.

132

'Glug . . . glug . . . glug . . . glug . . .'

That's the sound of you drowning, Pip. Want to hear it again?

OK:

'Glug . . . glug . . . glug . . . glug . . .'

The reason you're drowning is that the boat has sunk. So what are you going to do now? Your P.A.N.I.C. spell (if you still have it and can work it) will cast a bubble around you with enough air to keep you alive long enough to get to **124**.

Alternatively, there is a slim chance you may learn to swim terribly quickly (some people are fast learners when they have to be). Roll dice exactly as if you were rolling for your LIFE POINTS all over again. If your new score is better than your old, you may keep it as your new maximum and add swimming to your abilities. Finally, you might just get lucky. Roll 11 or 12 on two dice and you've made it. (Use your Luckstone if you have one.)

Providing you can survive this mess by any of the three possible methods, go to **124**.
If none of them worked, go to **14**.

133

Well, at least you're not dead. A little battered, perhaps, but definitely not dead. The only problem is that now you have to ask Merlin to fix the Minotaur's stupid great head.

'Don't forget your promise,' says the Minotaur as if reading your thoughts.

And the only way you can get to see Merlin during this adventure seems to be by getting yourself killed. They'd call that Catch 22 in your own time, Pip.

'How would it be . . .' you suggest hesitantly, '. . . if I promise to ask Merlin about your little difficulty the very next time I see him? I don't want to go all the way back now because I have a Brass Dragon to fight – if I can find it.'

'When are you likely to see him?' asks the Minotaur suspiciously.

'Next time I'm killed,' you say honestly.

'That shouldn't take too long in a place like this,' remarks the Minotaur. 'I'm a reasonable monster: I'll wait.'

'Thank you, Noble Minotaur,' you say politely.

'And,' adds the Minotaur in a sudden burst of generosity, 'once you have seen him, you may take the contents of my casket.' With which he impulsively forces the casket into your hands.

The casket will not open, however hard you try, until you have been once more to **14** and seen Merlin. (Or, if you are too stupid to get yourself killed, after you have gone back to the very start of this adventure.) But when you have fulfilled your promise – and not before – you may turn to **135** (make a note of the number) to find out what is in the casket before going on to the next Section you would normally reach from wherever you are. Got that? Good.

There are three passages out of the Minotaur cave. They lead to **114**, **128** and **137**. Take your pick.

Picking your way carefully over the bodies of dead Dwarves, you reach the bank of controls on the north wall. Inlaid in the gleaming metal floor beneath your feet is a blue metal plate. You test it carefully, but it seems secure to stand on. Before you are three large levers, surmounted by a notice in red. The notice reads:

PLACE KEY IN SLOT
BEFORE ACTIVATING LEVERS.

Beside the notice is a slot big enough to take quite a large key. The levers are numbered 1, 2 and 3. You can see that each one may be pushed upwards or pulled downwards. Make your choice carefully when you decide what to do with these levers because they will obviously determine the course of the remainder of your adventure. Here are your various options:

If you have a key to place in the slot, then the following results will arise:

Push all three levers up and go to **139**.
Push all levers down and go to **141**.
Push one lever up and two down and go to **144**.
Push two levers up and one down and go to **147**.

If you do NOT have a key to put in the slot, then the following results will arise:

Push all three levers up and go to **142**.

Push all levers down and go to **145**.
Push one lever up and two down and go to **148**.
Push two levers up and one down and go to **149**.

135

Chest 3 contains a scroll. This is what it says:

J FUIFMCFSU, NPOL BOE XBSSJPS, IBWJOH
CFGSJFOEFE UIF CFBTU XJUI UIF DPX'T IFBE
EP BUUFTU UIBU POMZ UIF LFZ XJUIJO UIF
DBTLFU XJMM QFSNJU BENJUUBODF UP UIF
MBJS PG UIF GJSFCSFBUIFST.

Which isn't very enlightening unless you can manage to decode it. Maybe there's something to help you in Chest 1. Quickly you throw it open and are promptly bitten by a large snake. Roll two dice to find out if the poison is lethal.

Score 2 – 4 and the poison courses through your veins like acid. Writhe in agony a little, then go to **14**.
Score 5 – 12 and you're naturally immune. Pop the silly snake back in its chest and try to decode the note.

As the Minotaur predicted, the remaining chests have vanished. The passages from the Minotaur cave lead to **114**, **128** and **137**.

Take your pick!

136

What a brave decision! A little greedy, perhaps, but brave.

Now for the bad news. The Medusa has 100 LIFE POINTS. She can turn you to stone any time she gets two successful hits against you in a row. She needs to roll an 8 or better to hit. If you decide to use your Invisibility spell during this fight, she can still get you, but she will need to make THREE successful hits in a row. Good luck.

If the Medusa kills you, go to **14**.
If you kill the Medusa, you will find you can comfortably carry treasure worth 200,000 Gold Pieces.
There are two passages leading out of the cave. They go to **138** and **128**. Take your pick.

137

This cavern is completely lined with metal! Floor, walls and ceiling! And the whole north wall is taken up with bank upon bank of truly massive machinery! This was never made by dragons! Or by anybody else in the time of King Arthur. If you weren't really a young person from the twentieth century occupying another body, you might be tempted to think it was magic. But you are a young person from the twentieth century, so you know perfectly well you are facing some strange sort of giant machine. But who made it? How did it get here? And what does it do? What a mystery.

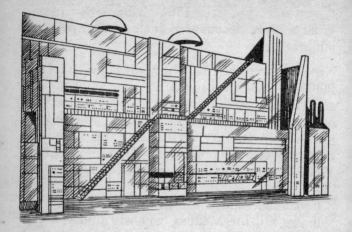

What a puzzle. What a glorious opportunity to poke around a bit and get yourself into no end of trouble!

You might be sorely tempted to walk directly to that control panel on the north wall were it not for one small thing. The machinery is being tended by no less than a dozen hunchbacked Dwarves of evil countenance. Twelve of them, Pip! Could even an adventurer of your reputation and experience fight them all? The choice is yours.

You may use your Invisibility spell here to get away safely. (Although that means going back the way you came, since there are no other exits to this place.)

You may try to creep away quietly. If so, roll two dice. Score 2 – 8 and you made it without

any of the Dwarves noticing. Score 9 – 12 and
they spot you and hurl themselves upon you
shrieking evilly, in which case you're stuck
with a fight so go to **131**.

You may hurl yourself upon the Dwarves and
hope to hack them to pieces. If so, go to **131**.

138

The passageway opens abruptly so-that you find
yourself standing on the rocky shore of a vast,
underground lake. There is no road around these
still, dark waters. But there is, at least, a rather
battered, leaky rowboat tied up only a few metres
away from you.

If you have previously discovered on this
adventure that you can swim, you might like to
try swimming the lake. (If you don't know
whether you can swim, don't risk it.) To
attempt to swim, go to **123**.

If you want to risk that rowboat (although it
does look very leaky) it will take you, via a
corridor, to **102**.

139

There is a hum of machinery. A vibration thrills
through your body. For a moment you feel dizzy,
disoriented. A spiral of light emerges from the
plate beneath your feet and coils around you. Your
head spins. You feel dizzy . . . Then blackness.

You are standing in an underground corridor of
worked stone, well lit by torches placed at

intervals in brackets on the walls. The metal-lined cavern has vanished. You are at a crossroads of sorts. The corridors run north-south and east-west. Fifty metres to the north is a door. Fifty metres to the south is a door. One hundred metres east is a door. One hundred metres west is a door. All doors are closed and there is no one else in the corridors.

Not much to go on, Pip, but where do you go from here?

Go north and go to **151**.
Go south and go to **154**.
Go east and go to **157**.
Go west and go to **141**.

140

Oh dear. You've just been fanged by a snake which was lying in Chest 1. (No, don't reach for your dice or writhe in agony, there's more.) Fortunately, like any sensible eccentric, you opened Chest 2 *first*. Inside was a small bottle clearly labelled SNAKE VENOM ANTIDOTE. Quickly you glug the antidote (which tastes revolting) and in moments you are feeling very much better, with the danger of Section **14** receding dramatically.

As the Minotaur predicted, the other chest and casket have vanished. Nothing more to do now but leave.

Exit passages from the Minotaur cave lead to **137**, **114** and **128**. Take your pick!

141

Darkness. And out of the darkness something hurls itself upon you. Something large and very nasty, not to say hairy. Fangs snap only centimetres from your throat. Talons rake against your chest. Vicious snarls and growls sound in your ears. All in all, it looks as if you're in for another fight.

The monster (or whatever it is) has 80 LIFE POINTS. It also has first strike against you. It hits

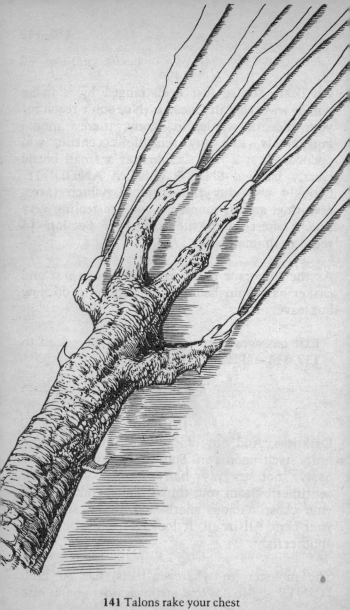

141 Talons rake your chest

successfully on a roll of 5 or better and does +2 damage. Go to it, Pip!

If the monster kills you, go to **14**.
If you kill the monster, go to **152**.

142

There is a hum of machinery. A vibration thrills through your body. For a moment you feel dizzy, disoriented. A spiral of light emerges from the plate beneath your feet and coils around you. Your head spins. You feel dizzy . . .

Then blackness.

Now go to **14**.

143

The casket contains a large key, which may be of some use to you if you survive the bite of the snake which is in the chest. Roll two dice to find out if the snakebite is fatal.

Score 2 – 5 and go to **14**.
Score 6 – 12 and you may retain the key without loss of LIFE POINTS.

As the Minotaur predicted, the remaining chests have vanished. There are three passages leading from this cavern. They lead to **137**, **114** and **128**. Take your pick.

144

Go to **108**.

145

There is a hum of machinery. A vibration thrills through your body. For a moment you feel dizzy, disoriented. A spiral of light emerges from the plate beneath your feet and coils around you. Your head spins. You feel dizzy . . .

Then blackness.

Now go to **14**.

146

Chest 2 contains a glass bottle clearly labelled SNAKE VENOM ANTIDOTE, which should come in handy if you're ever bitten by a snake. There is enough for one dose and it will absolutely neutralise the poison, leaving your LIFE POINTS exactly as they were before you were bitten.

Chest 3 contains a scroll. This is what it says:

J FUIFMCFSU, NPOL BOE XBSSJPS, IBWJOH CFGSJFOEFE UIF CFBTU XJUI UIF DPX'T IFBE EP BUUFTU UIBU POMZ UIF LFZ XJUIJO UIF DBTLFU XJMM QFSNJU BENJUUBODF UD UIF MBJS PG UIF GJSFCSFBUIFST.

Which isn't very enlightening unless you can manage to decode it. (And maybe not even then.)

As the Minotaur predicted, the remaining

chests have vanished. The passages from the Minotaur cave lead to **114**, **128** and **137**.

Take your pick.

147

There is a hum of machinery. A vibration thrills through your body. For a moment you feel dizzy, disoriented. A spiral of light emerges from the plate beneath your feet and coils around you. Your head spins. You feel dizzy . . .

Then blackness.

Go to **108**.

148

There is a hum of machinery. A vibration thrills through your body. For a moment you feel dizzy, disoriented. A spiral of light emerges from the plate beneath your feet and coils around you. Your head spins. You feel dizzy . . .

Then blackness.

Go to **14**.

149

There is a hum of machinery. A vibration thrills through your body. For a moment you feel dizzy, disoriented. A spiral of light emerges from the plate beneath your feet and coils around you. Your head spins. You feel dizzy . . .

Then blackness.

Go to **14**.

150

The casket contains a large key. Wonder where that might fit then? The chest is no help: it contains only a bottle clearly marked SNAKE VENOM ANTIDOTE, which may at least come in handy if you're ever bitten by a snake. It tastes horrible, but absolutely neutralises the poison, leaving your LIFE POINTS exactly as they were before the bite. There is enough in the bottle for one dose only.

As the Minotaur predicted, the remaining chests have vanished. There are three passages leading from this cavern. They go to **114**, **137** and **128**. Take your pick!

151

You exit the chamber into a tunnel cut through solid rock, which has all the indications of a natural fissure widened here and there to allow clear passage. One thing does occur to you quite strongly. Whatever that great machine was, whoever put it here, it has sent you to a different place . . . and there is no way back! Never mind, Pip: a brave adventurer can still go forward. Which is exactly what you do; until, quite suddenly, you reach another cavern.

You hesitate. This cave is very different from any you have seen before. It looks for all the world as if it had been formed from liquid rock, for the surfaces are smooth and the whole cave funnels downwards at a steep incline. You move forward cautiously, aware of the narrowing of the walls

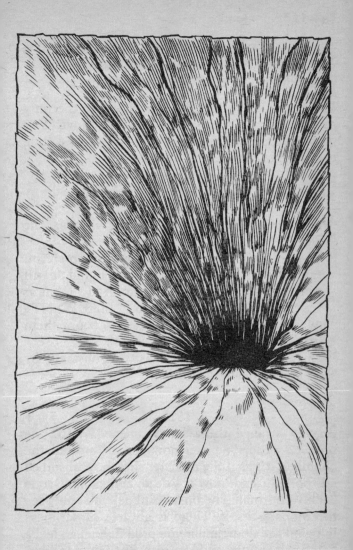

151 The cave funnels downwards

around you. Further and further you move, senses alert, as the funnel effect grows more and more pronounced. Oh, no! The funnel is blocked!

What now, Pip? The boulder blocking the only exit looks massive: far too large to move. You may have a try, of course (one try only), by rolling two dice.

> Throw 10, 11 or 12 to move the obstacle by brute force.
> If you fail in this throw, a Fireball will clear the way for you.
> If you have no Fireballs left, or would prefer to save them, try using the wand you found. It will gently dissolve the boulder into mud . . . but at the fearful cost of 25 of your LIFE POINTS (which may kill you, of course, so count them first otherwise you'll end up in **14**).
> Once you manage to get past this obstacle, by whatever means, go to **153**.

152

A very strange thing has happened. With the monster dead, you can now see all around the chamber. It's as if the monster somehow absorbed all the light and, now it's dead, things have gone back to normal. The only thing is, you can't see the monster itself. There is an area of darkness lying on the floor, and if you prod it you can feel a hairy pelt, talons and the rest. But you can't see anything. Looks as though you've killed some sort of magical Darkness Monster. Very odd.

But enough of philosophy. The chamber — and it's a proper chamber, not a cave — is pretty spartan. There is a heap of straw in one corner, presumably for the Darkness Monster to sleep on before you put it to sleep for good. Apart from that and a feeding dish, nothing else. Except the wand, of course.

The wand, which has a small leather thong at one end, is hanging from a nail on the west wall. It is made from ebony and tipped with jade. As you touch it, you can feel the familiar electric crackle of powerful magic, but neither waving it nor pointing it produces any observable result. Nonetheless, a wand is a wand, and magic is magic, so you tuck it away in the hope it may come in handy later.

There is only one door to this chamber. It leads to **151**.

153

A short passage, still descending, stops abruptly at the head of a flight of steps. They are crudely cut — very crudely cut — and worn smooth as if by the tread of many feet over aeons of time. But what feet have trod here? Not those of adventurers, surely, for only the strong, brave, intelligent adventurer could survive long enough to reach this spot: and such are rare. No, Pip, those steps have been worn smooth by some creature of the cave, some creature of darkness and evil intent.

Is that a sound you hear below? A gentle, sinister sound. A slither . . .

The creature sliding up the steps is green, a little more than two metres in length with blood-red eyes and a long, flicking tongue. A *very* long flicking tongue, bulbous at the end. *Flick!* That tongue snakes towards you like a whiplash. Roll two dice to discover if you are fast enough to avoid it.

Score 2 – 8 and you've managed to avoid it.
Score 9 – 12 and the tongue wraps around you like flypaper, trapping your arms and drawing you reluctantly into that gaping maw. Take time to be digested, then go to **14**.

Escaping the tongue doesn't mean you're out of the woods by any means. It simply gives you the opportunity to fight the Slither. The creature has no more than 20 LIFE POINTS but if it scores even a *single* hit, you are trapped and digested. The Slither strikes successfully on a roll of 8 or better.

If you are killed in the fight, go to **14**.
If you kill the Slither (and very good riddance if you do) go to **154**.

154

You step over the body of the Slither, already turning into evil-smelling slime, and make your way carefully down the steps into a smallish chamber. Another chamber, Pip, definitely man-made, but very old and long-abandoned by all appearances. The rotted remnants of a door hang by the entrance. The ceiling is half hidden by spider webs. An exit to the north leads into another passage, slanting downwards. But between you and the exit are some items of considerable interest: a chest, well preserved despite its age, and a newish-looking scroll dropped near the exit tunnel.

If you wish to read the scroll first, go to **170**.
If you wish to open the chest first, go to **156**.

155

It's a dead end! Would you believe anybody could do a thing like that? Fancy putting a complete dead end on a map! And you've trudged *miles* to get here. Afraid there's nothing else for it but to trudge miles all the way back again and try another route.

156

The chest is banded in brass, closed with a hasp. Inlaid on the lid is an ornamental and ornate design in gold leaf, surrounding a large carbuncle ruby. There seem to be several possible ways of opening the chest, Pip. You might, for example, simply flip back the hasp and try the lid.

If so, go to **171**.

You might, alternatively, consider that a chest of this type (which obviously holds something very important) must have a secret catch, probably triggered by the gemstone on the lid.

If so, press the gem and go to **164**.

Or you may by now be too impatient for these subtleties.

If so, use any convenient sword or blunt instrument to smash the chest open and go to **169**.

157

Aggressive little soul, aren't you? Well, since you decided to attack, you have the first strike at the little horrors. Which is maybe just as well.

Each Shape has only 4 LIFE POINTS, so one successful blow could kill it. But the problem is if you *don't* kill it first time, the Shape will blend gently into your body and remove 15 LIFE POINTS in the process. 15! Of course, the Shape destroys itself by blending, but that's not much consolation to you, is it? The Shapes attack in sequence. Until one is killed (either by you or by blending), the others will remain in the background and play no part in the proceedings. Go to it, Pip – and roll well!

If the Shapes kill you, go to **14**.
If you kill the Shapes, go to **162**.

158

That seems to have worked all right: the webs are cleared.

Go to **165**.

159

That seems to have worked all right: the webs are cleared.

Go to **165**.

160

The cavern you have entered is quite different from any other you have previously explored. Curious, crystalline structures are embedded in the various rock surfaces, scintillating softly in the torchlight, casting sapphire and emerald shadows that flicker like a magic flame.

It is a huge cavern, much larger than any other you have entered. The floor steps downwards in a series of broad, shallow terraces like some staircase constructed for a crippled giant. The final terrace sweeps away northwards, narrowing into a funnel which soars abruptly upwards forming an escape chimney through solid bedrock. The rank smell of dragons is everywhere.

A sudden plume of flame illuminates the entire cavern briefly before dying. In that brief instant, you catch a heart-stopping glimpse of the great fire-lizards: scores of them, hundreds of them, nesting in crevices, roosting on the high rock

outcrops far above your head, clinging to the rough walls like nightmare bats. Their red eyes watch you, silently. Not the entire Order of the Table Round could defeat this monstrous brood. Even the powerful magics locked within the Orb for which you risked your life may not be enough to hold them. Your every instinct screams at you to flee.

But you cannot flee. For there, on the lowest terrace, squatting hugely beside a blood-red crystal set upon a marble column, is the vast, unblinking bulk of the monster you have been sent to kill . . . THE BRASS DRAGON! The glinting amber eyes turn upwards to stare deep into your soul. *Hiss!* A tiny tongue of blue-green flame curls from the dragon's mouth. And as it does so, soundless words echo through your mind.

'WELCOME, PIP, ADVENTURER AND FAITHFUL SERVANT OF THE WIZARD MERLIN!'

Your heart skips a beat. This is telepathy! A *telepathic* dragon? No lore has ever spoken of the Brass Dragon as a mind-reader.

'NOT THE DRAGON, PIP. IT IS I WHO SPEAK TO YOU, MIND TO MIND.'

You look around, bewildered. Momentarily unmindful of the dragon brood within the cave, you call aloud, 'Who are you? Where are you?'

'I AM ETHELBERT, MONK AND WARRIOR, PIP, AN ADVENTURER LIKE YOURSELF, BUT

ONE WHOSE GOOD FORTUNE NOW SEEMS
TO BE ON THE WANE. AS TO WHERE I AM,
GOD'S WILL HAS PERMITTED THIS HELLISH
BRUTE TO WORK A STRANGE MAGIC
WHICH PLACED MY SOUL WITHIN THE
FOUL RED CRYSTAL SET UPON THE
PEDESTAL BEFORE YOU – WHEREIN I SHALL
BE DOOMED TO REMAIN FOREVER UNLESS
YOU HAVE THE STRENGTH TO SLAUGHTER
THIS DISGUSTING BEAST AND SHATTER
THE CRYSTAL TO FREE ME.'

'But how shall I kill the Brass Dragon?' you ask
desperately, for in truth, any small self-confidence
you ever had has now almost deserted you
completely.

'MAGIC, BRAVE PIP! MAGIC AND FORCE OF
ARMS. STRANGE FORCES ARE ABROAD IN
AVALON SINCE THE GATEWAY TO THE
GHASTLY KINGDOM OF THE DEAD WAS
OPENED BY THIS MONSTER. BUT I HAVE
GREAT CONFIDENCE IN YOU, PIP. TRUST IN
GOD AND STRIKE SURELY TO THE HEAD
WHEN YOU FACE THIS FOUL BEAST. BUT
FIRST YOU MUST RUN THE GAUNTLET OF
THE LESSER DRAGONS. MAY YOUR MYSTIC
ORB PROTECT YOU!'

And he's right, you know, Pip. Before you even
have a chance of getting yourself killed by the
Brass Dragon, there are those hundreds of other

dragons to deal with. So roll two dice, Pip: right now, before your nerve fails.

Score 1 – 9 and go to **163**.
Score 10 – 12 and go to **166**.

161

Dumb move, Pip – the webs hold you fast! Since there is no way of escape, you may as well go direct to **14**.

162

Look, Pip! There's an Orb at the bottom of the chest!

It rests on a purple velvet cushion beside a small inscribed plaque of polished brass. You bend forward to read the words; and the words are these:

THE ORB OF THE DRAGONMASTER

All natural-born firebreathing lizards are subject to the Orb. To activate its power, breathe upon its surface. If you be truly a Dragonmaster, no firebreather of natural species will attack you. If you be not truly a Dragonmaster, then the Orb may still protect you, although of this there can be no certainty until you put it to the test. If the firebreather be a lizard of the magic species, a Silver, Gold, Ebon or Brass Dragon, or the like, then the Orb will NOT have power over it, not even in the hands of a Dragonmaster.

What a find, Pip! Pity you're not a Dragonmaster, but at least now you have a chance of getting past the other dragons in this place before you meet old Brassy. So you take the Orb carefully from its velvet cushion and put it away safely, wondering who made it, and how long ago, and what race had Dragonmasters – a title unheard of in King Arthur's Avalon.

You search both chest and chamber thoroughly, but there is nothing more of interest here. The exit tunnel descends quite steeply into the bowels of the earth, and while it is little different from other tunnels you have passed along here, some instinct, finely honed by many dangers, tells you that now, as last, you are nearing your final goal. And it seems your instinct speaks truly. The rank stench of dragon grows stronger in your nostrils as a faint glow ahead gradually resolves itself into the luminous outline of another Cavern entrance. Beyond it, faint but unmistakable, comes the distinctive rustle of dragon wings.

Take a deep breath, Pip, and go to **160**.

You breathe upon the Orb, watching it cloud briefly, then flare into brilliant violet light. There is a rustling high above you as the great winged lizards react to the sudden luminescence. You take a deep breath and begin, heart thumping, to walk slowly forward. Will the Orb protect you? If the magic fails, not all your strength, not all your experience, not all your remaining spells will help you more than momentarily against a combined onslaught of these great beasts.

The dragons are restless, watching you intently. You reach the edge of the first terrace and step down. The Brass Dragon remains unaffected, as the plaque inscription warned you it would. But at least it makes no move towards you, content to wait until you reach its present level. Until you do so, the real danger comes from the other firebreathers. You hesitate, glance upwards. Dragon eyes glint evilly, reflecting the violet light of the Orb. One great beast takes off from a high ledge and plummets briefly towards you, then wheels, glides and returns to its roost high above.

You reach the second terrace and step down. In your hand, the Orb gently, quietly, begins to sing. The sound, soft though it is, echoes through the whole cavern. Pair by pair, the eyes that watch you begin to droop, begin to close. One by one, the great dragons tuck their heads beneath their wings and sleep. You have won the first round! The Orb has worked its powerful magic. Now all that remains is the most powerful dragon of them all, the huge brass monster that awaits you patiently below. You set down the Orb, still gently singing, and draw your faithful sword. Bravely, nimbly, you race across the remaining terraces to meet your fate in **172**.

164

The chest lid springs open! But at the same time, the gemstone flares briefly in a blaze of blood-red light, then crumbles into dust – leaving you minus 30 precious LIFE POINTS.

If this kills you, go to **14**.
If you survive, go to **169** to examine the open chest.

165

Oh, oh. There are small black *Shapes* flitting from the chest, Pip. Just little things, about the size of a

man's hand; maybe even a bit smaller. Six of
them, flapping up out of the chest like bats or
butterflies. Except they aren't bats or butterflies,
Pip. Or birds or moths or anything like that. They
aren't even solid! They just look like . . . well, like
shadows. They're probably nothing, Pip. Probably
not dangerous. They're probably nothing at all to
worry about. All the same, they're flitting towards
you.

If you decide to attack the Shapes, go to **157**.
If you decide to wait and see if the Shapes are
friendly, go to **168**.

166

You breathe upon the Orb, watching it cloud
briefly, then flare into brilliant violet light. There
is a rustling high above you as the great winged
lizards react to the sudden luminescence. You
take a deep breath and begin, heart thumping, to
walk slowly forward. Will the Orb protect you? If
the magic fails, not all your strength, not all your
experience, not all your remaining spells will help
you more than momentarily against a combined
onslaught of these great beasts.

The dragons are restless, watching you intently.
You reach the edge of the first terrace and step
down. The Brass Dragon remains unaffected, as
the plaque inscription warned you it would. But at
least it makes no move towards you, content to
wait until you reach its present level. Until you
do so, the real danger comes from the other

firebreathers. You hesitate, glance upwards. Dragon eyes glint evilly, reflecting the violet light of the Orb. One great beast takes off from a high ledge and plummets briefly towards you, then wheels, glides and returns to its roost high above.

You reach the second terrace and step down. The light in the Orb dims abruptly, flickers . . . dies! For one long, heart-stopping moment there is utter silence. Then Hell erupts above you as the mighty dragons swarm. Their great wings create a

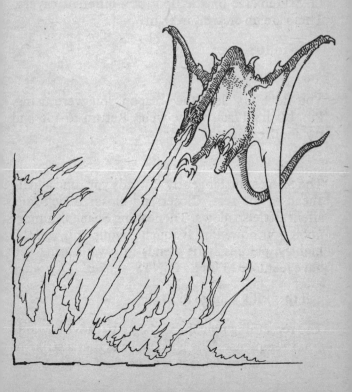

subterranean windstorm. The whole cavern is red with flame-breath.

You drop the Orb, which shatters on the ground, and bravely draw your sword. But as the monsters plunge towards you, you know this can be no more than a token fight. The first beast seizes you with angry talons and a strong voice echoes in your mind: 'YOU MUST TRY AGAIN, PIP! TRY AGAIN! TRY AGAIN . . .' And then all is claws and fangs and fire. You awake, minus half your LIFE POINTS, on the floor of a different cavern. There are no dragons in sight.

Go to **108**.

167

You have just lost the weapon you were using, Pip. It's held fast by the webs. Return to **156** and try another method.

168

The Shapes flutter gently towards you, one a little ahead of the rest. Closer and closer they come, silent little shadows. The leading Shape is almost upon you now, Pip. It touches your arm, gently. Lightly, painlessly, it blends into your arm. You have just lost 15 LIFE POINTS, sucker!

If this kills you, go to **14**.

The remaining five Shapes begin to move towards you in sequence. The good news is that a strike of only 4 or more damage will cause a single Shape to vanish. The bad news is that if you fail to hit first time, the leading Shape will blend into your body, causing 15 LIFE POINTS damage automatically, while the next one gets in line to take its turn.

If the Shapes kill you, go to **14**.
If you kill the Shapes, go to **162**.

169

It must have been many years since the chest was used – a tangled profusion of dusty spiders' webs makes it quite impossible to see inside. How do you tackle this one, Pip?

Brush them away with your hand? Go to **161**.
Cut them with EJ? Go to **167**.
Risk using one of your other weapons on them? Go to **158**.
Burn them away with a Fireball or similar spell? Go to **159**.

170

The scroll, which was plainly written very recently, reads:

'I, Ethelbert, monk and warrior, loyal subject of Arturus Rex, son of Uthur Pendragon and rightful Liege Lord of the Realm of Avalon, do hereby attest that by the grace of God and fleetness of foot, I have avoided the foul slithering creature which guards this accursed chamber and have, to my misfortune, explored the chest herein.

Be warned, you who may follow after me, that while the chest contains an artifact of inestimable value, it contains also death; and death in many forms. These I have discovered:

Within the hasp is a needle tipped with virulent poison.

Inlaid in the lid is a precious stone which, if pressed, will open the chest and place a curse upon the adventurer who touched it, causing the immediate loss of 30 LIFE POINTS.

Within the chest are webs, like unto spiders' webs – yet not natural webs, for these foul strands will hold firm any creature. Naught but a magic blade may cut them with impunity, else they may be burned through with magic fire.

Beneath the webs are creatures of the night, shadows no larger than the hand of a man, six in all, each so weak that a single blow might render its extinction, yet so strong that it can remove 15 LIFE POINTS in an instant.

Beneath these creatures is the treasure of the chest, a magical Orb which, so it is claimed, is the only means whereby an adventurer may survive in this foul cavern. But I for one do not believe this, trusting as I do in the grace of God. Thus have I left the Orb for those who follow after me.

This I aver.

Signed,   **Ethelbert**, monk and warrior.'

Now go to **156** to examine the chest.

171

A needle springs from the hasp to penetrate your thumb, which begins to sting almost instantly then quickly flares into a flame of agony, spreading in a massive swelling along your arm. Pretty nasty, huh? That needle was obviously poisoned, Pip. If you were not protected against poison, roll two dice.

Score 2–4 and you're naturally immune. Return to **156** and try another (hopefully safer) method of opening the chest.

Score 5–12 and you're dead. Go to **14**.

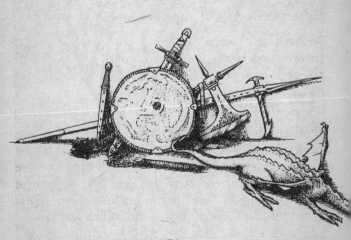

172

As you reach the lowest terrace, the Brass Dragon rears abruptly. Despite its bulk, the creature moves with truly alarming speed. It towers above

172 The Dragon's eyes glitter with hate

you, amber eyes glittering with hate. . .and intelligence. Dragon it may be, but this is no ordinary firebreathing lizard. This is a creature of strength and power and cunning. Now, face to face with it at last, you can see how the legend arose that it was born in Hell. An aura of powerful magic surrounds it, an aura of evil. All your strength, your skill, your ingenuity and your remaining spells must be thrown into the coming battle if you are to have the slightest possibility of success.

The Brass Dragon has 150 LIFE POINTS – far more than your own. It strikes on a roll of 5 or better and scores +5 damage on each successful hit with fang or claw. Each third hit, it breathes a plume of blue-gold fire which, if it strikes you, does +10 damage.

All your attack spells are effective against the monster. Invisibility is partially effective in that the Dragon can still sense your presence, but requires a roll of 8 or better to hit you while you remain invisible. Go to it, Pip, and calculate the outcome.

If the Brass Dragon kills you, go to **14**.

If you kill the Brass Dragon, go to **173**.

The vast carcass of the once deadly Brass Dragon lies twitching at your feet. Swiftly you step towards the glowing red crystal and smash it from its pedestal to shatter into sparkling fragments on the rocky floor.

A soundless burst of light! Standing before you in a stained and tattered robe, broadsword girdled at his belt, is a massive, bearded monk with flashing brown eyes, heavy brows and matted jet-black hair.

'By the holy toenail of Saint Paul, but it was cramped in there!' he rumbles. Then, bowing slightly, he introduces himself: 'Ethelbert, monk, warrior and faithful servant of Arturus Rex, son of Uthur Pendragon and rightful Liege Lord of the Realm of Avalon at your service.'

He hesitates, glancing at the Brass Dragon. 'Although, by the looks of things, you have little need of my services this day, Adventurer Pip, while I have every reason to be grateful for yours. But at least – ' He shrugs and settles the broadsword more comfortably at his hip. ' – I may show you the way out of here so that we may return to Camelot together to convey the news that the menace of the Brass Dragon is now over!'

173 The Brass Dragon lies dead at your feet

PIP TRIUMPHANT!

So it came to pass that on a day in Avalon, two strange, bedraggled figures made their way painfully from Dragon Cavern and along the secret paths which would lead them, eventually, back to Camelot. One was a huge, dark-eyed and black-bearded warrior monk. The other, smaller, slighter, but not one whit less impressive; a young but experienced adventurer whose name was surely destined to live forever in the annals of the Realm.

They travelled slowly, this oddly assorted pair, for both were weary from the efforts of various weird and dangerous adventures; and also because they dragged behind them a litter on which was stored much booty from the Dragon Caves. Not that Ethelbert, the monk, was much interested in treasure, of course; but Pip, the young adventurer,

was of a different philosophy and still smarted a
little at the loss of another treasure collected on a
different adventure.

The way back was uneventful, for they knew the
paths now and avoided such horrors as
Stonemarten Village. Nonetheless, it took them
several days to retrace their steps and return to
the point from which they had set out – or at least
the point from which Pip had set out. There in the
field was none other than Wandering Wanda, Pip's
favourite cow, looking sleek, content and full of
grass as if nothing untoward had happened in the
intervening time.

'What now, young friend?' asked Ethelbert, who
seemed to have attached himself to Pip since his
rescue from the magic crystal.

'I'm not entirely sure,' said Pip, frowning slightly.
'I suppose I should really report back to Merlin
and tell him the Brass Dragon is dead so that he
can go to the King and reclaim his pension. But to
tell the truth, I'm not exactly certain where to
find him. He has a log castle in the woods, but
when I last saw him he was in his crystal cave and
nobody knows how to reach him there.'

'But surely you do,' Ethelbert protested, 'since you
saw him there. Can't you remember the road?'

'I didn't take a road,' Pip explained (while being
careful not to explain too much). 'He brought me
to the place by magic.'

'Then perhaps he will bring us back there by magic,' Ethelbert suggested. 'Since this was your starting point, why don't we just sit down here and wait for him to do something about it. He is supposed to be a great magician, after all – the greatest in the Realm. He must realise very soon that we are here with good news for him.'

And so the two companions sat in the field, guarding their treasure, with nothing better to look at than Wandering Wanda, and waited. And waited. And waited. . .

Meanwhile, in the Crystal Cave (which really did smell so much better than the stench of Dragon Cavern), the greatest magician in the Realm was having a little trouble with his latest spell.

It was a simple enough piece of magic – or should have been – based on the well-tried alchemical principle of changing lead to gold. Since his pension had been docked, the problem of stockpiling a little gold had become acute for the Wizard, so that in desperation he had purchased a consignment of lead from a merchant and hired a team of dray horses to drag it to the secret entrance of his present hiding place. The transaction, including the hire of the horses, had taken almost every penny he had, but he was certain he could recoup his investment (at a vast profit) once the alchemical operation was complete. Over the course of a week, he had personally carried the lead, a little at a time, into the crystal cave and piled it untidily in the middle of the floor near the makeshift furnace which formed an important part of the alchemical operation.

For those with an interest in such things, he was using a process called the Chymical Marriage of the White Queen and the Green Dragon, which had nothing to do with marriage, dragons or queens, or even chemistry for that matter (which just goes to show how confusing alchemy can be). Rather, it involved melting down the lead in the

furnace then adding to the molten mixture a
collection of rare herbs and spices while waving a
wand and chanting the words of a particular spell.
It was something Merlin had done quite often
during his student days when he was learning the
first steps of magic in the Druid College at
Llandogo. Then, under the direction of his tutors,
it had always worked perfectly. Now, for some
reason, it kept going wrong. The lead changed all
right, but not into gold. Each time the ringing
echoes of the spell died down within the cave, the
lead turned into steamed pudding.

The seventh time this happened, Merlin (who
didn't even like steamed pudding) flew into an
uncharacteristic rage, overturned the furnace and
stamped away to another wing of his crystal cave,
briefly determined out of bad temper and pique to
place a blight on the kitchen garden of the
Archbishop of Canterbury. (Merlin's dislike of the
Archbishop and the Archbishop's mutual dislike
of Merlin were well known in Avalon, although
no one – including the two old men themselves –
could remember how the trouble between them
actually began.)

Although one would not, of course, wish ill on an
Archbishop, it was fortunate that Merlin did lose
his temper at that time. For while searching for
his blight wand in a cupboard, he came across his
crystal ball (mislaid for almost a week) and
therein noticed young Pip in the company of a

Merlin looks in his crystal ball

cow and a rough-looking fellow in monk's robes. Beside them was a crudely made litter, apparently piled high with all sorts of treasure and assorted rubbish. But the important thing was that the canvas covering had slipped a little to reveal the head of the Brass Dragon.

Merlin stared short sightedly into the crystal for a moment, scarcely able to believe his eyes. Then he did a very strange (and possibly magical) thing indeed. He performed a whooping tap-dance all around the crystal cave.

ADVENTURES NEW

'There will be a banquet, of course,' said Merlin thoughtfully, 'and a tournament and so forth with myself as Guest of Honour – and a place for you above the salt, young Pip, in recognition of the part you played in ridding the Realm of this monster.'

'May I bring my friend Ethelbert?' Pip asked.

'If he cleans himself up a bit,' Merlin said expansively. His eyes glazed again as he followed inward thoughts. 'I shall have my pension restored; very possibly even increased, since Arthur tends to be quite generous in situations like these. You can keep any treasure you've collected, Pip. Buy yourself a castle or something, possibly a new farm for your adoptive parents. The King may even be moved to elevate you to the aristocracy. You're a bit young, but who knows. I estimate we will have quite a while to enjoy ourselves before the trouble starts.'

'Trouble?' Pip blinked.

'Oh yes,' said Merlin. 'You did a sound job on the

Brass Dragon, no doubt about that. But the Gateway is still open.'

'The Gateway?' Pip echoed.

'To the Ghastly Kingdom of the Dead,' Merlin snapped testily. 'I did tell you. As long as that stays open, the Realm is in all sorts of danger. Still, you can always sort that out when you've got your breath back, enjoyed your banquet and so forth. Mark you, the business with the Brass Dragon is only a sideshow compared with the dangers you'll face when you go into the Ghastly Kingdom of the Dead.' He smiled. 'But I have great faith in you now, Pip. Yes, yes indeed. I'm quite sure if anyone can manage it, you can. So don't worry about a thing. Just slip back to your own Time for a little rest and I'll call you again when I need you to tackle the Ghastly Kingdom.'

Yes. That's going to be your next adventure, Pip. Your next triumph, if you can survive it. A dreadful place, of course, but I'm certain you can manage it.

And I'll call you for the job. Yes indeed.

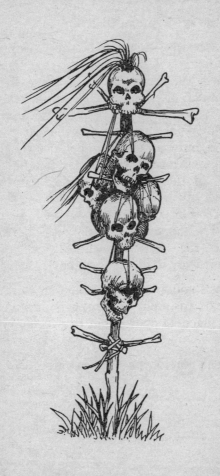

DREAMTIME

DREAMTIME

This Section is used ONLY when you decide to Sleep during an adventure. If the dice direct you here, follow these Rules:

1. You enter Dreamtime with your LIFE POINTS at the exact level they were when you decided to Sleep.

2. You enter the Dreamtime without armour or protection of any sort.

3. You enter the Dreamtime without magic or weapons of any sort, save those which may be given you in a specific encounter.

4. You may take nothing back from the Dreamtime.

5. Any LIFE POINTS lost in the Dreamtime are deducted from your actual LIFE POINTS. If you are killed in the Dreamtime, you are really killed and must go directly to the dreaded Section **14**.

Now enter Dreamtime by throwing two dice and going directly to the dreamtime section indicated by your score.

If you survive, return to the Section where you decided to Sleep.

Dreamtime Sections

2. You are facing a small, cigar-shaped flying creature which dives at you incessantly. Although it does not touch you, each pass causes a ripple to pass over your brain with the automatic loss of 5 LIFE POINTS. The creature is a Brain Teaser. It has 15 LIFE POINTS and strikes first. Fight quickly!

3. You are being chased through a graveyard by a Vampire. If the ghastly creature catches you, you die! Already your legs are turning to jelly. Will you escape? Roll the Vampire's STRENGTH using two dice. Then roll your own STRENGTH, again using two dice. Compare STRENGTHS. If the Vampire has scored more than 5 points higher than you, he will catch you. . .

4. You are in the empty Banquet Hall of a strange and rather beautiful castle. On the table before you are two chalices, one of crystal, the other of bronze. One contains wine, the other poison, but you have no way of telling which is which and you must drink from one of the chalices. Test your LUCK now by rolling two dice. A score above 6

indicates that you are lucky enough to choose the correct chalice. A score of 6 or below indicates that you have drunk the poison, in which case roll two more dice and subtract the total from your present LIFE POINTS.

5. You are trying to escape from the turret of a high tower and have climbed out through a narrow window in the hope of scaling down the outside wall. Although there are good toeholds, the surface is very slippery. Roll two dice to discover if you fall: score under 6 and down you go! If you find that you do fall, roll two more dice to find out if you fall on solid ground or in the moat. Score under 6 and you fall on solid ground for the loss of 10 LIFE POINTS. Score 6 or above and you fall in the moat with NO loss of LIFE POINTS, but you must roll two more dice to see if you can swim. Score under 6 and you can't swim: you drown and die.

6. You are walking in a beautiful walled garden enjoying the summer sunshine when you are attacked by a swarm of bees. Each bee sting costs you 1 LIFE POINT. Roll one die to discover how many bees actually manage to sting you.

7. One of Merlin's spells has gone badly wrong and turned you into a stick of celery. You are now growing quietly in a vegetable patch. It is not such a bad life since you have cabbages

and cauliflowers to talk to, but Merlin's goat has broken through the fence and is munching his way towards you. Roll one die to discover if he likes celery. Score below 6 and he will nibble away 5 LIFE POINTS before passing on to eat all Merlin's carrots.

8. You are jousting with the Black Knight, a fearsome villain with 25 LIFE POINTS. You are wearing armour which deducts 5 from any damage scored against you. His armour is better and deducts 6 from damage scored against him. The lance used by the Black Knight adds 10 to any damage he scores in the joust. Your lance, however, has been blessed by the Archbishop of Canterbury and adds 12 to any damage you score. King Arthur rolls two dice to decide who will strike the first blow. If he scores 2–6, then the Black Knight goes first. If he scores 7–12 then you will go first.

9. You are in a gloomy corridor facing a large, hairy Sleep Monster. You have no weapons or armour, but nearby are two caskets. You have time to open only one of them before the Sleep Monster attacks. Roll one die. Score 1–3 and you find a magical dagger which dispatches the Sleep Monster instantly. Score 4–6 and the casket you open is full of sleep gas. This means you must sleep again and make new rolls to find out if you are headed for the DREAMTIME.

10. You are hunting boar in the forest and are armed with a bow and seven arrows. Each arrow scores a straight 10 points of damage if it hits, and you require to throw better than 6 on two dice in order to hit. You enter a clearing and discover a huge Ogre about to eat a comely maiden. You have time to fire all seven arrows before the Ogre can possibly reach you. The Ogre has 40 LIFE POINTS and is so strong he scores +15 damage with the huge club he carries. You have seven chances to kill him before he reaches you and (because he is slow) one additional chance to finish him off with your bare hands before he thumps you with his club.

11. Following a disagreement with King Arthur about whether or not the world is flat, you have been cast without food or water into a deep, dark dungeon. How long you remain there depends on the results of your next die roll. For each point scored up to a maximum of 6 you remain one day – and lose 1 LIFE POINT – before the King relents.

12. You are on a high mountain top engaged in a magical battle with an evil Sorcerer who has occupied the top of a neighbouring mountain. In this battle you hurl gigantic waves of magical blue fire at one another. So long as both of you hurls a wave, the magic neutralises and no damage is done. But sooner or later one of you is going to run out of waves. Roll one die to find out how many

waves the enemy Sorcerer has left and one die to find out how many you have left. The one with the most waves reduces the opponent's LIFE POINTS to half their current total and wins the battle.

Rules of Combat

To Find Your Starting LIFE POINTS
1. Roll two dice and add the scores together.
2. Multiply the result by 4.
3. Add any PERMANENT LIFE POINTS gained in other *Grailquest* adventures.

To Strike an Enemy *
Roll a 6 or higher on two dice.

To Damage an Enemy
1. Check how many points you rolled above the number needed to strike.
2. Subtract this from your enemy's LIFE POINTS.

To Knock Out an Enemy
Reduce his LIFE POINTS to 5.

To Kill an Enemy
Reduce his LIFE POINTS to zero (0).

Your enemies use the same method to attack you, as you roll dice for them.

Armour & Weapons
1. Using armour subtracts from damage scored against you.
2. Using weapons increases the damage you score.
3.* You are permanently equipped with *EJ*: Needs a roll of only 4 on two dice and causes 5 extra damage points. If you have adventured through *The Castle of Darkness* you also have the *Dragonskin jacket*: Deducts 4 from damage done to you.

To Restore Lost LIFE POINTS
1. *Sleep:* You can sleep any time except when fighting. Roll *one* die. If you score 1-4, turn to *Dreamtime*. If you score 5 or 6, LIFE POINTS are restored equal to rolling two dice.
2. Other LIFE-restoring methods are given through the adventure.

N.B. LIFE POINTS cannot be restored to above your Starting total – except through Experience.

EXPERIENCE POINTS

1. 1 EXPERIENCE POINT is gained for each fight or puzzle won or solved.
2. 20 EXPERIENCE POINTS = 1 PERMANENT LIFE POINT. 10 of these can be taken into future adventures.

To Test for a Friendly Reaction

Roll one die *once* for your enemy and one die *three* times for yourself. If you score *less* than your enemy, he is Friendly. Proceed as if you had won a fight.

Attack Magic

1. Each spell thrown costs 3 LIFE POINTS whether or not it is successful.
2. No spell can be thrown more than three times. Once thrown it is used up whether or not it has been successful.
3. A 7 or higher must be thrown for a spell to work.
   Spells
   PANIC: Subtracts 4 extra points from damage done to you.
   POW: Adds 10 points to damage scored.
   PILL: Causes opponent to miss three turns in combat.
   PAD: Causes 10 damage points to an enemy at any range.
   PIP: Gives immunity to poison, when taken *before* poisoning.
   PIN: Neutralises an enemy spell cast on an object.
   PIR SQUARED: Gives you two turns in succession throughout a given combat round.
   INVISIBILITY: Makes you invisible. Can be used only *once* in Sections indicated. Costs *15* LIFE POINTS.
   FIREFINGERS: Spell can be thrown successfully *once* only to give 10 Bolts, each scoring 10 damage. Unused Bolts can be fired at any later time.
   FIREBALLS: Spell can be thrown successfully *once* only. Gives two Fireballs, each scoring 75 damage. If unused, can be taken forward and fired at any later time.

Repeat Journeys

On repeat attempts at the adventure, any enemies previously killed remain dead. Any treasure collected is lost unless you are told otherwise.